DEDICATION AND INAUGURATION

OF THE

VANDERBILT UNIVERSITY.

NASHVILLE, TENNESSEE,

OCT. 3, 4, 1875.

Nashville, Tenn.:
PUBLISHING HOUSE OF THE METHODIST EPISCOPAL CHURCH, SOUTH.
1875.

FACULTIES OF THE UNIVERSITY.

LANDON C. GARLAND, LL.D., CHANCELLOR.

DEPARTMENT OF PHILOSOPHY, SCIENCE, AND LITERATURE.

L. C. GARLAND, LL.D., Professor of Physics and Astronomy.

NATHANIEL T. LUPTON, M.A., LL.D., Professor of Chemistry.

J. C. GRANBERY, M.A., D.D., Acting Professor of Mental and Moral Philosophy.

MILTON W. HUMPHREYS, M.A., Ph. D., Professor of Greek.

B. W. ARNOLD, M.A., Adjunct Professor of Latin.

EDWARD S. JOYNES, M.A., LL.D., Professor of Modern Languages and English.

ANDREW A. LIPSCOMB, D.D., LL.D., Professor of Philosophy and Criticism.

JAMES M. SAFFORD, M.A., M.D., Ph. D., Professor of Mineralogy, Botany, and Economical Geology.

ALEXANDER WINCHELL, LL.D., Professor of Zoölogy, and Historical and Dynamical Geology.

WM. LEROY BROUN, M.A., LL.D., Professor of Mathematics.

BIBLICAL DEPARTMENT.

T. O. SUMMERS, D.D., *Dean,* Professor of Systematic Theology.

A. M. SHIPP, D.D., Professor of Exegetical Theology.

J. C. GRANBERY, D.D., Professor of Practical Theology.

R. M. MCINTOSH, Professor of Vocal Music.

LAW DEPARTMENT.

THOMAS H. MALONE, M.A., *Dean of the Faculty,* Professor of Commercial Law and Insurance, Equity Law, Jurisprudence of the Courts of the United States, and Pleading and Practice in Civil Cases.

W. B. REESE, *Secretary of the Faculty,* Professor of the Law of Real Property, Criminal Law and Procedure, Torts, and International and Constitutional Law.

E. BAXTER, Professor of the Law of Domestic Relations, Agency, Partnership, Corporations, Evidence, Wills, and Executors.

MEDICAL DEPARTMENT.

THOMAS MENEES, M.D., *Dean of the Faculty,* Professor of Obstetrics.

JAMES M. SAFFORD, M.D., *Secretary of the Faculty,* Professor of Chemistry.

PAUL F. EVE, M.D., Professor of Operative and Clinical Surgery.

WILLIAM T. BRIGGS, M.D., Professor of the Principles and Practice of Surgery.

THOMAS L. MADDIN, M.D., Professor of the Institutes and Practice of Medicine.

WILLIAM L. NICHOL, M.D., Professor of the Diseases of Women and Children, and of Clinical Medicine.

VAN S. LINDSLEY, M.D., Professor of Physiology.

THOMAS A. ATCHISON, M.D., Professor of Materia Medica and Therapeutics.

THOMAS O. SUMMERS, JR., M.D., Professor of Anatomy and Histology.

JOHN H. CALLENDER, M.D., Professor of Psychological Medicine.

CHARLES S. BRIGGS, M.D., Demonstrator of Anatomy.

CONTENTS.

PREFACE.

THIS volume is meant to be the beginning of a series, to be issued annually. Addresses on Commencement and other special occasions, Baccalaureate Sermons, and such Scientific Discourses and Lectures as may be delivered in the Course of Instruction, and be thought proper for publication, will constitute the material for future volumes of the VANDERBILT UNIVERSITY Series, of uniform edition with the present one.

It is proposed, in this way, to make a contribution to general literature that shall possess permanent value. Unlike the justly celebrated Bampton Lectures, and other similar courses of lectures which generous founders have provided for, the subjects of this and following volumes will be found to be various—suited to the times in which they appear; but like them, it is to be hoped, in this—the best thoughts of the best minds on problems most worthy of public attention. A history of current thought, and a defense of truth against present existing objections, will, therefore, be a feature of these publications. The first volume will be accepted as a fair specimen of this style.

The *Alumni* of the older institutions of learning cannot but regret that productions similar to those herein and hereafter to be preserved—productions of orators and essayists of the first order, stimulated to their highest effort by appreciative surroundings—have never been given to the world. If published, they exist now only in fugitive pamphlets, scarcely to be found, or are bound up with other miscellaneous works of their authors, and not readily accessible.

The candid reader will require no apology for being presented, along with graver matter, with the connecting incidents of the Dedication and Inauguration Exercises which are peculiar to the beginning. And he will also be pleased to have, as a part of this Preface, some account of the foundation of the Institution of which this volume is a kind of first-fruits.

The University owes its foundation to the munificence of Mr. CORNELIUS VANDERBILT, a citizen of New York, who, on the 27th of March, 1873, made a donation of Five Hundred Thousand Dollars for this purpose, to which he afterward added more.

The acknowledged want of the means of a higher Christian education than could be obtained within their bounds led several Annual Conferences, in the year 1871, to appoint delegates to a Convention, to "consider the subject of a University such as would meet the wants of the Church and country." The Convention met in Memphis, January 24, 1872, and was composed of delegates from Middle Tennessee, West Tennessee, Alabama, Mississippi, Louisiana, and Arkansas.

The Convention was in session four days, and adopted a plan for a University. Under the plan a Board of Trust was nominated and authorized to obtain a Charter of Incorporation, under the title of "The Central University of the Methodist Episcopal Church, South."

A liberal Charter was obtained that year, and the Board of Trust met January 16, 1873, and completed its organization. By-laws were adopted, and agents appointed to solicit funds. A University in fact, as well as in name, had been determined on; in the words of the Convention, "An institution of learning of the highest order and upon the surest basis, where the youth of the Church and the country may prosecute theological, literary, scientific, and professional studies to an extent as great, and in a manner as thorough, as their wants demand." The members of the Convention were not ignorant of the vastness of the undertaking, nor of the magnitude of funds essential to success. Their judgment in the matter was expressed in the form of a resolution declaring that One Million of Dollars was necessary to perfect their plans and realize fully their aims; and so important was it, in their estimation, to avoid an abortive effort, that they refused to authorize steps toward the selection of a site and the opening of any department of the University until the public showed itself to be in sympathy with the movement by a valid subscription of Five Hundred Thousand Dollars.

Such, however, was the exhausted condition of the South, and so slow its recuperation under the disorganized state of its labor, trade, and governments, that the first efforts to raise funds showed the impossibility of the enterprise. The yearning desire of our people seemed destined to disappointment for this and following generations, and the well-laid scheme was already—in the judgment of some of its warmest friends—a failure. At this crisis Mr. VANDERBILT came to their help. In his sympathy for a people struggling to revive their fortunes, and to secure for their posterity the highest blessing of Christian civilization, he stepped forward and, by his princely gift, gave form and substance to the plan. The Board of Trust, in accepting the donation, as an expression of gratitude resolved to change the name of the projected Institution to VANDERBILT UNIVERSITY; and on their petition the Charter was so amended. Thus the VANDERBILT, like the more successful institutions of learning in our country—as Harvard, Amherst, Dartmouth, Cornell, Peabody—inherits the name of its founder.

The following important paper—the original proposition of Mr. VAN-

DERBILT concerning the University—is here inserted as the fundamental fact in its history:

NEW YORK, *March* 17, 1873.

TO BISHOP H. N. MCTYEIRE, *of Nashville:*

I make the following offer, through you, to the corporation known as *The Central University of the Methodist Episcopal Church, South:*

FIRST—I authorize you to procure suitable grounds, not less than from twenty to fifty acres, properly located, for the erection of the following work.

SECOND—To erect thereon suitable buildings for the uses of the University.

THIRD—You to procure plans and specifications for such buildings, and submit them to me; and, when approved, the money for the foregoing objects to be furnished by me as it is needed.

FOURTH—The sum included in the foregoing items, together with the "Endowment Fund" and the "Library Fund," shall not be less in the aggregate than Five Hundred Thousand Dollars ($500,000); and these last two funds shall be furnished to the corporation so soon as the buildings for the University are completed and ready to be used.

The foregoing being subject to the following conditions:

FIRST—That you accept the Presidency of the Board of Trust, receiving therefor a salary of Three Thousand Dollars per annum, and the use of a dwelling-house, free of rent, on or near the University grounds.

SECOND—Upon your death, or resignation, the Board of Trust shall elect a President.

THIRD—To check hasty or injudicious appropriations or measures, the President shall have authority, whenever he objects to any act of the Board, to signify his objections, in writing, within ten days after its enactment; and no such act is to be valid unless, upon reconsideration, it be passed by a three-fourths vote of the Board.

FOURTH—The amount set apart by me as an "Endowment Fund" shall be forever inviolable, and shall be kept safely invested, and the *interest* and *revenue*, only, used in carrying on the University. The form of investment which I prefer, and in which I reserve the privilege to give the money for the said Fund, is in seven per cent. First Mortgage Bonds of the New York Central and Hudson River Railroad Company, to be "registered" in the name of the corporation, and to be transferable only upon a special vote of the Board of Trust.

FIFTH—The University is to be located in, or near, Nashville, Tennessee.

Respectfully submitted: C. VANDERBILT.

At a called meeting of the Board of Trust, on March 26, 1873, the above letter, containing Mr. VANDERBILT's proposition, was duly presented, and the following resolutions were adopted:

RESOLVED, That we accept with profound gratitude, this donation, with all the terms and conditions specified in said proposition.

RESOLVED, That, as an expression of our appreciation of this liberality, we instruct the Committee hereinafter mentioned to ask the Honorable Chancery Court to change the name and style of our corporation from *The Central University of the Methodist Episcopal Church, South,* to THE VANDERBILT UNIVERSITY; and that the Institution, thus endowed and chartered, shall be from henceforth known and called by this name.

Mr. VANDERBILT afterward added to his original gift, without any material change of conditions. In a letter to Bishop McTYEIRE, dated New York, March 24, 1874, he says:

> Referring to your letter of the 17th inst., I beg to say that the plans you have shown me, as therein stated, are approved.
>
> As you express some doubt whether the "Endowment Fund" of Three Hundred Thousand Dollars can be preserved, if these plans are fully carried out, and as you consider such a Fund of vital importance to the success of the Institution, I have decided to add One Hundred Thousand Dollars ($100,000) to the whole Fund.

An eligible site was selected in the West End of Nashville—a plat lying in an oblong square, and containing seventy-four acres. Ground was broken for the main edifice of the University September 15, 1873, and the corner-stone was laid April 28, 1874. By October, 1875, the various buildings and apparatus were in a condition of readiness for opening the University; and a Library of about six thousand volumes had been collected.

The main building contains Chapel, Library and Reading-room, Museum, Laboratories, and Lecture-rooms, and Offices for Professors. In all its arrangements it is ample and well ventilated, built according to the most approved models, and suitably furnished, and warmed throughout by steam. On the grounds are eight professors' houses, recently constructed; also, a commodious building, capable of accommodating thirty or forty young men, appropriated to the use of a certain number of students in the Divinity School.

These structures, together with Observatory, outhouses, and accommodations for the Janitor and other *employés* of the University, present, at convenient distances from the principal building, a group of eleven brick and an equal number of frame buildings. The grounds have been well inclosed and suitably improved with roads and walks, water and gas pipes, and the planting of about one thousand trees.

While these expensive improvements were in progress a financial panic fell upon the country: banks closed, and even Government works were suspended; but Mr. VANDERBILT steadily furnished the funds, and there was no delay, at any time, on that account.

The Professor of Chemistry, who formerly studied at Heidelberg with Bunsen, returned to Germany, after his election, for the purpose of investigating the latest methods and instruments of scientific teaching, and to purchase a complete outfit for his Department. The Chancellor inspected the leading institutions of the country before making out the *Curriculum* of the University, and in April went abroad to procure, on personal inspection, the Physical and Astronomical Apparatus. The United States revenue laws allowing such articles to be imported free of duty, by an institution of learning for its own use, this arrangement was economical, in view of the large outlay for these purposes, and also secured the latest improvements in scientific furniture.

The situation of Nashville could not fail to commend itself to the comprehensive views and practical judgment of such a man as Mr. VAN-

DERBILT when founding an Institution of Learning for Southern youth. In the midst of a food-producing country, it meets the first conditions of good and cheap living. The climate is salubrious, equally free from the rigor of Northern winters and the debilitating heat of lower latitudes. Central between East and West, its railroad system makes it accessible to students from every part of the country, and especially is it convenient to the teeming populations of the Valley of the Mississippi.

It is allowable, in this connection, to allude to the effect of this benefaction upon public sentiment. It was without precedent. A citizen of the North, Mr. VANDERBILT could have found there ready acceptance of his gift, and built up an institution rivaling those which abound in that wealthier and more prosperous section of the country; but to the South he looked, and extended to her people what they needed as much as pecuniary aid—*a token of good-will.* The act, timely and delicately as munificently done, touched men's hearts. It had no conditions that wounded the self-respect, or questioned the patriotism, of the recipients. The effect was widely healing and reconciling, as against any sectional animosities which the late unhappy years had tended to create. A distinguished statesman remarked: "Commodore VANDERBILT has done more for reconstruction than the Forty-second Congress." And when the life-size portrait which adorns Central Depot in New York, as duplicated by the skill of Flagg, the original artist, was unveiled in the Chapel at Nashville, thousands looked upon it then, and look on it still, as upon the face of A FRIEND AND BENEFACTOR.

It happened unavoidably—when was it ever otherwise?—that the cost of *completing* plans of such magnitude outran the most careful estimates. No architect or builder can foresee all the items of expense that are developed as such a work progresses. So it was in this case; but the considerate generosity of Mr. VANDERBILT was equal to the occasion, as the following letter shows, on his transmitting to the Board the Endowment Fund ($300,000), being notified of their readiness to take charge of it:

No. 25 WEST FOURTH STREET, NEW YORK, December 2, 1875.

BISHOP H. N. MCTYEIRE, *President Vanderbilt University, Nashville, Tenn.*

MY DEAR SIR:—I have looked over, in a general way, the statement of expenditures made and to be made on account of the at first called "Central University of the Methodist Episcopal Church, South," which name was subsequently changed to "VANDERBILT UNIVERSITY"—the compliment of which action, on the part of your Board of Trust, I fully appreciate.

Your statements show that the expenditures already made, with the additional ones necessary to be made to cover all the cost of grounds, buildings, books, and apparatus, and all salaries and incidental expenses to the first day of December, 1875, so that the Institution will, on that day, be entirely free from all debt and obligations, amount to $392,831 46. Of this amount you have already drawn on me for, and I have paid, $360,000. For the balance, $32,831 46, you may draw on me whenever, and as fast as, the items, to the payment of which it is applicable, can be paid off.

At this point I desire to say that I am fully satisfied as to the faithfulness and, also, the judiciousness with which the expenditures have been made, and with the clearness with which they have been classified and stated.

When I made my proposition, under date of March 17, 1873, to give not less than $500,000 to the Institution, it was, as you will remember, expected that at least $300,000 of that amount could be preserved as an "Endowment Fund," which was to be kept "forever inviolate and safely invested, and the interest or revenue thereof, only, used in carrying on the University."

Under the representations made in your letter of March 17, 1874 (just one year after my proposition was made), that the cost of completing the erections, and their suitable appurtenances, would, under the plans that had so far been worked upon, impair to some considerable extent the originally-intended amount of the "Endowment Fund," I agreed, in my letter to you dated March 24, 1874, to "add $100,000 to the whole fund"—making it $600,000—upon the condition that not over $300,000 (including what had already been paid) should be used for the grounds, buildings, etc., and that at least $300,000 should be reserved as an "Endowment Fund," to be kept inviolate, as provided in my original proposition.

When I saw you at Saratoga Springs, last summer, you stated that the completion of the work would impair the "Endowment Fund," even as fixed in my second offer; and I said that whatever obligations were incurred on account of the work must be paid off, so that the Institution would be absolutely free from debt, even although it required *all* the "Endowment Fund," my opinion being that no *real* fund of that nature could exist so long as any indebtedness was outstanding against the Institution.

When the amounts you have herein been authorized to draw for shall have been paid, so that the Institution will be clear from all debt to the first day of December, 1875—making, as hereinbefore stated, an aggregate of $392,831 46—it will leave but a trifle over $200,000 for the "Endowment Fund," instead of $300,000, which last, from the outset and all through the progress of the work, was considered a matter of very great, if not of vital, necessity.

Upon a careful review of all the circumstances, and consideration of the objects sought to be accomplished by the Institution, and feeling that its beneficial operations should not be restricted, now that its material structures are so well adapted to success, I have decided to make an additional contribution, sufficient to bring the "Endowment Fund" up to the full amount of $300,000, as originally contemplated—thus making an aggregate contribution of $692,831 46.

[Here follows a description of the sixty Bonds, of $5,000 each, sent as the invested Endowment, seven per cent., payable semi-annually.]

And now that I have fulfilled my undertakings in this matter, I beg, in closing these statements, to say that to you, my dear sir, who have labored so actively and so earnestly in carrying out the plans for the University—and have labored so efficiently, too, as its inauguration within thirty months shows—and who will, as the President of the Board of Trust, have the chief responsibility in respect of the accomplishment of the educational purposes for which it was undertaken, I tender my personal expressions of extreme regard, trusting that the healthful growth of the Institution may be as great as I know it is your desire and determination to make it. And if it shall, through its influence, contribute, even in the smallest degree, to strengthening the ties which should exist between all geographical sections of our common country, I shall feel that it has accomplished one of the objects that led me to take an interest in it.

Very truly yours, C. VANDERBILT.

Dedication and Inauguration.

THE Dedication and Inauguration Exercises of the VANDERBILT UNIVERSITY took place October 3, 4, 1875.

At ten o'clock on Sunday morning, October 3, the Chapel of the University being filled, the Dedication exercises opened with a voluntary by the Choir—followed by Hymn 77 (tune, Lenox):

Young men and maidens, raise
  Your tuneful voices high:
Old men and children, praise
  The Lord of earth and sky:
Him Three in One, and One in Three,
Extol to all eternity.

The univer'sal King
  Let all the world proclaim;
Let every creature sing
  His attributes and name!
Him Three in One, and One in Three,
Extol to all eternity.

In his great name alone
  All excellences meet,
Who sits upon the throne,
  And shall forever sit:
Him Three in One, and One in Three,
Extol to all eternity.

Glory to God belongs:
  Glory to God be given,
Above the noblest songs
  Of all in earth and heaven:
Him Three in One, and One in Three,
Extol to all eternity.

Prayer was offered by Bishop McTyeire, and the Lessons were read by Bishop Doggett.

Hymn 155 (tune, Coronation) was sung:

All hail the power of Jesus' name!
  Let angels prostrate fall:
Bring forth the royal diadem,
  And crown him Lord of all.

Ye chosen seed of Israel's race—
  A remnant weak and small—
Hail him, who saves you by his grace,
  And crown him Lord of all.

Ye Gentile sinners, ne'er forget
  The wormwood and the gall:
Go, spread your trophies at his feet,
  And crown him Lord of all.

Let every kindred, every tribe
  On this terrestrial ball,
To him all majesty ascribe,
  And crown him Lord of all.

O that, with yonder sacred throng,
  We at his feet may fall!
We'll join the everlasting song,
  And crown him Lord of all.

Then followed the Sermon by Bishop Doggett:

THE DYNAMICS OF CHRISTIANITY; OR, ITS SYSTEM OF MORAL FORCES.

"The powers of the world to come." Heb. vi. 5.

In the economy of God, we stand in intimate relations to two worlds at the same time: the world of sense and the world of faith—the world temporal and the world spiritual—the world present and "the world to come."

The object of Christianity is to aggrandize our natures, to elevate us above the pressure of the world of sense, to make us acquainted with the spiritual and eternal world, and to bring us into contact and conformity with it. It possesses a perfect capacity to accomplish this object. Our text announces its capacity, in speaking of "the powers of the world to come."

I propose to discourse to-day, by the help of God, upon what I may call *the dynamics* of Christianity: in other words, upon the moral forces which it employs in order to accomplish its object—the laws by which its grand economy is regulated. Let us, however, contemplate,

I. The wonderful dispensation of which the text speaks—the new order of things to which it refers—in the phrase, "the world to come."

It is not, in any absolute or exclusive sense, the future state which is spoken of, as commonly understood, and as apparently indicated in the terms themselves. We have a strictly parallel allusion in the fifth verse of the second chapter of this Epistle, decisive of this interpretation, in which the author says: "For unto the angels hath he not put in subjection the world to come, whereof we speak?" It is manifest that he had not been speaking directly or exclusively of the future state at all.

Of what, then, had he spoken? and of what does he speak in the language of the text? Unquestionably, of the Christian dispensation—the kingdom of heaven—the world of redemption, established by Christ in the midst of the present world. This dispensation is a special, divine organization, instituted for the purpose of introducing into our world a system of restorative agencies, to reach and to rectify our ruin.

We pause a moment to delineate, in some sort, this extraordinary department of the divine administration—to set forth several of its distinctive features.

One of them is its intrinsic character. In this respect it is purely spiritual, as contradistinguished from every form of temporal government. It is spiritual in its genius, in its subjects, and in its methods of operation. Said Jesus Christ, "My kingdom is not of this world."

It is distinguished by peculiar external exhibitions. It embodies itself, of necessity, in such visible forms as are expressly declarative of its existence and results—such as evince its true and living realization amongst men. So much it assumes, and no more.

It is denoted by its comprehensive range. It includes within its appropriate scope the present life, with all its interests; the invisible world, with all its population; and the future state, with all its issues. What an empire, therefore, is "the world to come" in its extent!

Its designation is remarkable. Why is it described as "the world to come?" Evidently, in part, in respect to prophecy, the fulfillment of which the author was showing in its establishment. He was writing, from the prophetic point of view, to those who held and reverenced the prophecies. It was the coming age of the prophets—the coming kingdom to which they all referred. It is so called in respect, also, to the settled expectation of the Jewish nation previously to, and at the time of, writing. However mistaken they were as to the character of the Messiah's reign, the great national idea was the establishment of his future kingdom in the world. It was, in fact, "the world to come" to them—the world which had actually begun to the apostle—the transition period from the old to the new. At the same time, it was literally and really "the world to come" in respect to its development and perpetuity, viewed especially from its then incipient stage. It was, truly, the coming world—a world ever to come, and never to end.

"The world to come," thus defined, is essentially and intensely present at all times. It is all around us; we are in the midst of it; it interpenetrates the world of sense and sin in which we live.

Withal, it is real and permanent. Nothing is so real; nothing is so permanent. All else is a comparative illusion. In reference to it St. Paul says: "We look not at the things which are seen, but the things which are not seen: for the things which are seen are temporal; but the things which are not seen are eternal." They alone abide. The visible world is the shadow of the invisible. It is the curtain which hangs between the spectator and eternity. Presently the curtain will rise; the wondrous scene will burst upon us, and we shall find ourselves in a contracted theater, environed with the startling realities of an unchangeable existence. The visible world is the scaffold—the temporary substructure—upon which we now stand. The pending catastrophe shall dissolve it; but we shall survive, and be transferred to the imperishable foundations of "the world to come."

We proceed now to consider more particularly what we have taken occasion to denominate,

II. The dynamics of Christianity. The term is not chimerical: it is the literal rendering of δυνάμεις, the word employed in the original text. Christianity has its dynamics as well as natural science, and in advance of it. It signifies powers, forces, active agencies, energetic influences.

Christianity, as a system, is replete with moral forces—with active agencies—with which it effects its benign purposes. It is not a negative, inert organization, consisting of a faultless but impotent ideal of conceivable excellence. It is infinitely potential. It possesses the inherent capacity of self-subsistence, of victorious aggression, and of indefinite reproduction.

We speak habitually of the laws of nature—of the forces by which its vast and varied machinery is regulated—of the vital energies by which it performs its functions; and we speak correctly, so far as phenomena are concerned. These categories comprise our philosophy of nature. The apostle speaks with stronger warrant, and with better propriety, of "the powers of the world to come"—the forces which operate in the sphere of revealed religion—those higher laws which pervade the realm of redeeming grace, and which constitute the sum of its exhaustless efficiency, and of its imperial grandeur.

It remains for us to inquire, briefly, what those forces are. This inquiry plunges at once into the region of the supernatural. It cannot be avoided; it is a necessity and a joy. The very phrase, "the world to come," indicates a supernatural order of things actively existing, and about to be fully displayed. The whole condition of things with which Christianity brings us in contact is grandly supernatural. If it is not supernatural, it is nothing—it is a myth and a delusion. Emasculate it of this quality, and it collapses like any other mythological bubble. But it is something—a very decided something—an irresistible and a mysterious something. It is a fact—a tremendous, a transforming fact—in the world's history, an impracticable fact to its opponents; in a word, it is a supernatural fact. It cannot be emasculated, and it will not collapse; and we are as precisely conscious of its supernatural character as we are of the facts of nature. The whole hue and cry on this subject is a preposterous fallacy. For myself, I will not surrender my consciousness, or my common sense, to its exorbitant exactions.

Let us now attempt to define some of "the powers of the world to come." We commence by remarking that they do not include those temporary miraculous endowments which distinguished the primitive movement of Christianity—those charisms, or special gifts, which attested its introduction into the world. Though necessary, they were incidental and transient. The "powers" here claimed are inherent in and inseparable from it, and, as the context assures us, may be *tasted*, or experienced, as the disciplinary and subsidiary process of our salvation. They pertain to the constitution of the kingdom of God; they comprise the whole class of moral agencies which enable a man to work out his own destiny—the entire volume of hallowed influences of which the Scriptures give us information. We enumerate amongst them,

1. The Truth-power. "The world to come" is the world of truth. It is replete with truth. Truth is its fundamental element, not only in the sense of the apprehended reality of that world, but in the sense of the explicitly formulated expression of the truth which pervades it. That truth is not an abstraction of the human intellect: it is the revealed word of God, of which Jesus Christ, in appealing to his Father, said, "Thy word is truth"—the pure, the absolute, the eternal truth, in respect to finite intelligences. It is the law of their natures—the universal standard of moral excellence. Nor is the truth, thus expressed, only an infinitely perfect moral code: it possesses, likewise, the quality of an infinitely energetic moral force, perpetually working out its salutary results with imperial authority and efficiency. It is "quick and powerful" in asserting its benignant prerogative, not merely when first realized, but ever afterward, intrenching itself in the understanding, revealing itself in the consciousness, and unfolding itself in the character, of all who are the subjects of it. This, then, is one of "the powers of the world to come"—one of those sublime forces which, without intermission, perform their functions in the realm of grace.

2. Another of these forces, and no less wonderful in its effect, is the Life-power—the power of imparting and sustaining life in its original import. The kingdom of Christ

is the empire of life, as well as of truth. He is its infinite repository, and its unfathomable fountain. "In him was life" from all eternity, and he is "the life" to all eternity. The world of redemption was constituted that life, through him, might be restored to "the dead in trespasses and in sins," and that they might be reunited to the living universe. From him it is ever flowing, and actively exerted by the Holy Ghost upon all who are in fellowship with him. It transforms and elevates, purifies and glorifies, them. It works mightily, and pulsates with vigorous strokes, in the souls of believers. It sends its vitalizing current, without cessation, throughout the world of redemption. It is the "well of water springing up into everlasting life;" it is the "pure river of the water of life, clear as crystal, proceeding out of the throne of God and of the Lamb," rolling its stream of blessing through avenues of paradisiacal trees, laden with fruits whose taste is joy, and luxuriant with foliage whose touch is health. This divine life circulates, with spontaneous activity, in all the members of that great family of which Christ is the Head, "changing them into the same image, from glory to glory, even as by the Spirit of the Lord." And, to complete its transcendent object, its resistless impulse will reach the domain of natural death, and startle and evoke from its shades the slumbering bodies of the saints, and invest them with the attributes of a robust and gorgeous immortality. "Then shall be brought to pass the saying that is written, Death is swallowed up in victory;" then will the scene of its desolation be reversed, and the vision of life from the dead burst upon the new heavens and the new earth.

See truth, love, and mercy in triumph descending,
  And nature, all glowing, in Eden's first bloom;
On the cold cheek of death smiles and roses are blending,
  And beauty immortal awakes from the tomb.

What a marvelous force is life in the natural world! How productive, how multifarious, how irresistible! How richly it replenishes and embellishes the face of nature! How irrepressible, for example, is the outburst of vegetable life when the earth presents her responsive bosom to the genial rays of the vernal sun! Were repression possible, its recoil would shatter the globe into atoms. How much grander is the Life-force in the kingdom of God, by which redeemed humanity, in obedience to its laws, after "groaning and travailing in pain together, will be delivered from the bondage of corruption into the glorious liberty of the sons of God!"

3. One of "the powers of the world to come" is the Light-force which it contains—its capacity to enlarge and illuminate the horizon of the soul. It is a world of light, as well as of life, in correspondence with the order of God in the physical creation: "For God, who commanded the light to shine out of darkness, hath shined in our hearts, to give the light of the knowledge of the glory of God, in the face of Jesus Christ." Christ is the central Light—the Sun of righteousness—in the kingdom of grace; and those who obey him "walk not in darkness, but have the light of life." The light of this kingdom is the light of divine knowledge—of a clear and vivid apprehension of the great questions of "life and immortality brought to light by the gospel," compared to which all other questions are but "vanity and vexation of spirit." This knowledge is not speculation, but demonstration added to demonstration in an ever-ascending scale of indefinite progression. The kingdom of Christ is the school of inspired knowledge—the august temple of infallible wisdom—in all that appertains to the moral perfection and eternal destiny of man. The entrance into it is a passage "from darkness to light;" and to continue in it is to "walk in the light, as Christ is

in the light." What an unspeakable happiness, to enjoy correct ideas of divine truth—to expand and expatiate with its endless discoveries—to gaze, with unblenching eye, upon its undiminished effulgence!

But divine illumination is more than a happiness: it is a power. Natural light not only reveals the forms of life by which we are surrounded: it is necessary to their existence and development. So the light of "the world to come" is one of its essential forces: it quickens and stimulates the growth of Christian manhood, and adorns it with its beauteous proportions. Gentle as it is, it puts the moral machinery into motion; it starts and stirs the faculties of the soul into a holy and healthy activity. If ever the maxim that "knowledge is power" was true, it is sublimely true in the world of Christianity.

4. Again, to accomplish its purposes, it employs the Love-power. Supreme love to God and universal love to man is the cardinal impulse—the constraining motive—of the gospel kingdom; it is the sovereign affection of the regenerated soul; it is the foundation of obedience, the sum of morality, the compendium of the commandments. It is the climax of all moral forces, the consummation of all precepts, and the harmony of all relations. In loving God, we adore his perfections, delight in his service, and promote his glory; in loving man, we honor his nature, pity his miseries, and seek his happiness. Love is, therefore, equally the law of attraction and the law of action in "the world to come."

5. Besides, it brings into constant requisition, as one of its effective agencies, the power of Hope. The influence of hope upon human activity and endurance is an acknowledged force in the enterprises of life. It sheds an alluring luster on its pathway, and flickers even in its expiring moments.

> Hope springs eternal in the human breast:
> Man never is, but always to be, blest.

The kingdom of God is the theater and the asylum of hope: it is never delusive there. In that sphere it is "as an anchor of the soul, both sure and steadfast, and which entereth into that within the vail; whither the forerunner is for us entered, even Jesus, made a high-priest forever, after the order of Melchisedec." The world of redemption is thronged with objects of desire, and enriched with the rewards of obedience. Hope rises to the contemplation and anticipation of them, and fires the soul with unquenchable ardor in their pursuit. It fortifies with patience and animates with exertion all its faculties, to obtain "the prize of the high calling of God in Christ Jesus."

6. In this category of moral forces we assign a place to the law of sanctified reciprocity. The effect of it on the character and condition of the Christian is a proof of its intensity and its value. It is "the bond of perfectness" which unites into one vast brotherhood the whole Church of the living God, identifying each with all, in the contest for victory. When one approaches the gate of the kingdom, he is solitary and desolate; he leaves the world of sin and sinful men behind him; he needs new sympathies, new affections, and new associations. When he enters, Christianity brings him into instant contact and companionship with "the general assembly and Church of the first-born, which are written in heaven—with the spirits of just men made perfect," and with all on earth who are making "their calling and election sure." He is surrounded with their presence, supported by their fellowship, encouraged by their example, and assisted by their prayers. What a wealth of advantage is comprised in the communion of saints! What a moral force resides in the collective strength of the household of faith!

7. The Christian system includes amongst its vital forces a special arrangement to meet the emergencies of the Christian life. It does not precipitate us into the arena of duty and of danger, and abandon us to the perils of the strife: it subsidizes in our behalf the aid of divine grace, and the interposition of divine providence. The life of faith is a struggle exhausting in its labor, and a battle fearful in its conflict. God is not so much a spectator of our fortunes as an omnipotent Friend in our distress—working in us of his good pleasure, and enabling us to work out our salvation. He hastens to our relief. His seasonable assistance is one of the constitutional provisions of "the world to come," in order to secure our ultimate success. We may, therefore, "come boldly unto the throne of grace, that we may obtain mercy, and find grace to help in time of need."

8. It subordinates to its benevolent purposes the angelic power—the ministry of the unfallen angels. Throughout their celestial gradations they are rendered subservient to the welfare of the saints, and perform official functions in their behalf. If we cannot define their functions, we are acquainted with their office and relations: "Are they not all ministering spirits, sent forth to minister for them who shall be heirs of salvation?" Every member of the imperial hierarchy, from the highest archangel to the lowest functionary in their resplendent ranks, contributes the measure of his capacity to promote the salvation of the children of God. Do they not fan our fevered brows with ambrosial plumes? Do they not whisper cheering words in the hour of dismay? Do they not rush into the breach, to protect and to rescue, in the moment of danger? Are not our departing souls "carried by angels into Abraham's bosom?"

9. Finally, "the world to come" is pervaded by the ex-

ecutive power of the divine administration. It is a perfectly-organized government, over which Jesus Christ himself presides. It is plenipotentiary, self-subsistent, and self-sufficient. It will take care of itself and of its subjects, and will survive all obstacles. It will redeem all its pledges, and will indemnify the losses sustained in its service by an "eternal weight of glory."

These, my brethren, are some of "the powers of the world to come, whereof we speak"—some of those moral forces which enter into and augment the plenitude of resources which pertain to the kingdom of grace, and which it employs to facilitate, and to secure for us, "an abundant entrance into the everlasting kingdom of our Lord and Saviour Jesus Christ."

Our theme to-day is fertile in conclusions.

It defines the position of man in the scale of being. He is the paragon of the creation, the heir of two worlds, and the connecting link between them. How magnificent is man, viewed in his relations to the visible and invisible universe! How he towers aloft, as he stands revealed in the light of that manhood and monarchy with which God has endowed him!

It shows the interest awakened in the heavenly places in his behalf. He is the focus of a thousand merciful contrivances; he is the object of an amazing system of agencies to rescue and to raise him to the platform of a majestic maturity and a glorified immortality; he is the center of a circle radiant with divine benedictions, and replete with benevolent instrumentalities.

Our subject foreshadows the grade of moral culture which awaits his earnest concurrence. What transformations, what purity, what dignity, will crown his faithful exertions! The chief of sinners may become the elect of God. The soiled mantle of earth may be exchanged for the clean and white linen of the saints, and he may walk the streets of the New Jerusalem as a king and a priest unto God forever.

It behooves him to place himself in contact with the divine apparatus prepared for his benefit. He must invoke its power, and adjust himself to its salutary influence. He must arouse himself to the greatness of his destiny, and assert his manhood in the achievement of it.

Our subject defines the responsibilities of those who are engaged in the education of youth. The cultivation of the intellectual nature must recognize and respond to the cultivation of the moral nature. We have seen the divine arrangements for the one: we must adopt corresponding methods for the other. The robustness and completeness of the human character consist in their harmonious combination. There must be no antagonism between them; otherwise, the result will be a distortion, and not a model.

Our subject indicates the legitimate career of this great institution. This is neither the time nor the place to eulogize its munificent benefactor: that commendation will be deferred until to-morrow. The VANDERBILT UNIVERSITY arises under the auspices of Christianity—amidst the prayers and blessings of the Church. It must vindicate its vocation by fidelity to its claims; it must link its fortunes to the plastic "powers of the world to come." The Church must settle, in the seats of learning, the true correlation between science and religion, and rescue Christianity from the charge of incompatibility with the higher culture of humanity. A great vocation this—a grand problem to be worked out! Happily, we enjoy to-day the evidences of this design. Christian services anticipate the scholastic inauguration; Christian ideas and Christian faith assert their prerogatives in advance; and side by side with halls of literature and science stands this beautiful Christian temple, to offer a sanctuary and an asylum to Christian truth.

Our theme evinces the inexhaustible grandeur of Christian thought. Rapid as is the advancement of natural science, and brilliant as are the discoveries of human research, the progress and development of Christianity transcend them all; for, while the one unfolds the wonders of the natural world, the other discloses the glories of "the world to come," and elicits the rapturous exclamation, "O the depth of the riches both of the wisdom and knowledge of God! how unsearchable are his judgments, and his ways past finding out!"

God grant that the benefits of a solid education in science and literature, imparted in this institution, may be consecrated by the experience of a sound conversion, and by a growth in grace and in the knowledge of our Lord Jesus Christ! "Now unto him that is able to keep us from falling, and to present us faultless before the presence of his glory with exceeding joy, to the only wise God our Saviour, be glory and majesty, dominion and power, both now and ever. Amen."

After the Sermon was sung the following Dedication Hymn (tune, Duke Street):

Father Almighty! hear our cry!
Sovereign of all on earth, on high:
Lord God of power and might, thou art
The strength and hope of every heart!

Eternal Wisdom! Light have we
Only as it beams forth from thee:
Let the refulgent rays divine
On our poor darkling spirits shine!

Fountain of Love! Without thy grace
Earth is a dreary, cheerless place:
Thy all-comprising peace impart,
Spirit Divine, to every heart!

Great Three in One! Now from above
Give power, give wisdom, and give love,
As thus we consecrate to Thee
With joy our University!

Lord, let thy work to us appear,
Thy glory to our children here;
Our work shall then established be
To us and our posterity.

Patrons and benefactors bless—
To teachers, students, give success:
We pray in faith, assured thou wilt
Shine forth upon our Vanderbilt!

After Prayer by Bishop PAINE, the Doxology was sung, in Old Hundred:

Praise God, from whom all blessings flow;
Praise him, all creatures here below;
Praise him above, ye heavenly host;
Praise Father, Son, and Holy Ghost.

The Benediction was pronounced by Bishop DOGGETT.

IN the afternoon, at three o'clock, the congregation reässembled, and after a voluntary by the Choir, Hymn 771 (tune, Howard) was sung:

How shall the young secure their hearts,
  And guard their lives from sin?
Thy word the choicest rule imparts
  To keep the conscience clean.

When once it enters to the mind,
  It spreads such light abroad,
The meanest souls instruction find,
  And raise their thoughts to God.

'Tis like the sun, a heavenly light,
  That guides us all the day;
And through the dangers of the night,
  A lamp to lead our way.

Thy word is everlasting truth;
  How pure is every page!
That holy book shall guide our youth,
  And well support our age.

Prayer was offered by the Rev. CHARLES F. DEEMS, D.D., Pastor of the Church of the Strangers, New York.

The Lesson was read by Bishop WIGHTMAN.

Hymn 794—being a part of a Hymn written by Charles Wesley for the Kingswood School, founded by John Wesley in 1748—was sung in Creation, as follows:

Come, Father, Son, and Holy Ghost,
  To whom we for our children cry;
The good desired and wanted most,
  Out of thy richest grace supply!
The sacred discipline be given
To train and bring them up for heaven.

Unite the pair so long disjoined,
  Knowledge and vital piety:
Learning and holiness combined,
  And truth and love, let all men see,
In those whom up to thee we give,
Thine, wholly thine, to die and live!

Then came the Sermon by Bishop WIGHTMAN, as follows:

CHRIST THE CENTER AND BOND OF THE UNIVERSE.

"By Him all things consist." Col. i. 17.

The context fixes, beyond doubt, the meaning of the word "Him" in the text: it is, and can be, none other than the Lord Jesus Christ.

"Consist" is a word transferred from the Latin to our tongue, from the Greek equivalent of which we derive the word *system;* the idea in both being that of a "standing together"—a mutual dependence, one part upon another, each for all—the whole scheme pervaded by a controlling idea giving law to the arrangement. The conception of the text seems to be that Christ is the great center of unity and bond of connection between the grand departments of universal being; or, as Bengel long since expressed it, "all things in him have come together into one system." As Mediator, God manifested in the flesh, he is the *nexus* between the mighty objective whole and the unseen, infinite, eternal Father.

This system embraces Nature—the whole region of necessitated things, controlled by cause and effect—the realm of the conditioned.

It embraces, also, Humanity, as in part supernatural, because a spiritual, immaterial essence—the soul—is united to a material organism—the body. This is the sphere of the rational, ethical, immortal.

It comprehends, also, the realm of purely spiritual intelligences, of which revelation gives us distinct intimations in angel and archangel, principalities, dominions, and powers.

This is the scope of the *all things* in the text.

This universal whole, in the verse preceding the text, is affirmed, distinctly and peremptorily, to have been *created* by the Son, who is the image, the visible manifestation, of Deity. Since he is Creator, so this universal whole has in him subsistence, consistence. Hence his own sublime affirmation, "I am Alpha and Omega, the first and the last."

Look at Christ in the sphere of nature.

As the Son of God, he created this planet that it might be part of his vast scheme of order, might be the fit platform for the training of man, of mind, for a glorious future immortal destiny. For man's use, not he for its, were formed its soils and ores, its coal-fields and forests; for him are its atmosphere, its light, its waters; for him its laws were established, its wheels roll. All its arrangements are but means, never ends. It is, and ever must be, unintelligent: showing forth the glory of God, but never comprehending its own purpose; eternally thing, never person; to be used by intelligent mind, itself forever unconscious.

Into this world came the Son of God, taking upon him the condition of man—"born of a woman, born under the law, that he might redeem" the fallen race. His object was, by coming down into humanity, to lift humanity to God. It has been nobly said that "it is the especial glory of our race that it should have furnished that point of contact at which God has united himself not to man only, but also through man to his own universe, to the universe of matter and of mind."

He is in the sphere of cause and effect in nature; but is it wonderful that at his birth a great company of angels sang, "Glory to God in the highest, and on earth peace, good-will toward men?" Is it wonderful that at pleasure he controls the wheel-work of nature, creating food for thousands, turning water into wine, walking the foam-crested waves of the sea, healing diseases by a touch, saying to stormy winds, "Be still," and by the mandates of his will plucking the prey from the grasp of death? Well might nature, so to speak, have come and fallen at his feet, and confessed him its absolute Lord and Master!

Behold him in the sphere of the human *supernatural!* The true man, according to St. Paul, is the *inner* man. The spirit belongs not to the region of nature's cause and effect; it is not subject to nature's fixed necessitations: it moves in the sphere of spontaneity, and is autonomic and free—the will capable of *originating* action—above necessity, by reason of the power of self-determination vested in it.

Its law is not the law of cause and effect in nature, but the "moral law"—that moral law within which, with the starry heavens above, are the two things which Kant, the greatest of German philosophers, said overwhelmed him with astonishment and awe. This spiritual essence, as free and ethical, is capable of knowing the right and doing it; yet it feels a strange proclivity to the wrong. Fallen from original rectitude, depraved man acknowledges, nevertheless, the imperatives of duty. Conscience is his dread prerogative. He may be that terribly magnificent thing, a sinner; hence the strange discords within him, partly angel, partly demon, with capacities wonderfully lofty, with tastes as wonderfully sordid—a lost Pleiad, broken loose from the heavenly attractions. Under sin, manifestly; listen to the groan which now and then breaks from his agonized spirit: "O wretched man that I am! who shall deliver me?"

Into this region Christ comes as a Deliverer. His vicarious, sacrificial death has solved the problem how God can be just and justify the ungodly. Even as he unites in his own person the manhood and the Godhead, he is mighty to suffer, and "mighty to save." "When we were enemies, we were reconciled to God by the death of his Son." In Christ's redemptive-work behold the great, stupendous *consideration* of reconciliation! The love of the Father to the Son, who thus bore the malediction due to the sinner, is an ineffable, unfathomable love; it goes into all the provisions of redemption, into all the plan of salvation. Redemption once accomplished, there needs, indeed there can be, no other altar, no other blood, no other priest—none, none—to come between the sinner and his Saviour. The way is open to the holiest by the blood of Christ.

Now, beyond cavil, this is supernatural work *for* the element in humanity which is above nature's fixed necessitations. It is God that justifieth, not man working out some such result by self-development. And so is the gracious work wrought *in* man. To them who receive Christ, who believe on his name, "he gives power to become the sons of God." This power renews the soul; this power brings the affections into harmonic play with the dictates of conscience; the result of its operation is being "born of God." And thus adoption comes with justification. But all this is supernatural work. Christ is the binding, unifying principle. Without him, there is no redemption, no pardon, no sanctification, no final glorification. Abiding in him by constant faith, we have real and constant fellowship with the Father. The central point of the supreme desire and aim of an immortal spirit is reached in this union with God, and all perturbations cease.

But *man needs reconciliation with himself.* In Christ he finds this.

His reason and his faith are reconciled in Christ. As God-man, Christ is the union of the absolute with the relative. He is the living realization of the loftiest of the reason's ideals; he is the supreme manifestation of love to the sentiment of the heart. He that leaves the principles of the doctrine of Christ, and goes on to perfection, reaches that shining summit at which, to adopt the noble expression of Dr. Arnold, "faith is reason leaning on the bosom of God."

The *sense of obligation* and the *freedom of love* are reconciled. There is law; but the soul, pardoned, renewed, and bathed in the light and warmth of the love of Christ, cries, "O how *love* I thy law: it is my meditation all the day!" Not that Christ has obeyed for him, and made virtue a thing of proxy: the obedience is real, but loving, cordial, constant, because Christ's gospel has become a "law of liberty." Let the sense of responsibility be deep and urgent, but take with it the word of Christ, applicable to all occasions of duty, all emergencies, all suffering: "My grace is sufficient for thee; for my strength is made perfect in weakness." Over and beyond all natural force of will—all the strength which comes from a bracing self-discipline—we find in Christ the "enabling principle" of obedience, and then we "can do all things through Christ that strengtheneth us."

Prayer and effort are harmonized. In the last analysis prayer is the expression of absolute dependence on God for every thing; it is the abandonment of all self-assertion, all self-trust. But if you wish to find the fountain-head of all the noblest achievements for the good of humanity—of the unnumbered activities by which Christendom has been beautified and blest—of the time, labor, self-sacrifice, that have been freely given for the maintenance and propagation of truth, go to the closet where the pleading, beseeching prayer, made potent with God through the advocacy of the crucified, ascended, and glorified Son, asks for help in the time of need. Ay, the banners which wave in triumph over all battle-fields are banners which have been laid in humble devotement on the altar of an incarnate God.

Thus, too, the loftiness of hope and the lowliness of humility coëxist in the heart which has enthroned Christ, the man of sorrows, the Lord of glory.

How beautifully might the great truth of the text be shown by referring you to the harmony and true relation, the one to the other, of a life in the flesh, and a life by the faith of the Son of God!

How forcibly might it be shown that all competent, worthy, and noble conceptions of *education* must find, as the complement of what is secular and merely intellectual, the distinct recognition of Christ's influence—his teachings, his grace—as the "bright, consummate flower," the crown and glory of the whole educational process!

But I have not time to carry your thoughts much farther along the line of illustration—so fruitful, so boundless, so joy-inspiring—suggested by the thesis of the text. I must not attempt to show how Christ, as the great connecting force, binds man to man. Certainly, I have no capacity of thought or expression, no wing of inspiration, to lift you to the starry altitudes of my theme, in any attempt to show you how this Christ of yours will bind the most exalted intelligences of the wide and populous universe to God—to man, God's human, redeemed, immortal offspring. It is enough to repeat the glowing words of St. Paul: "That in the dispensation of the fullness of times he might gather together *in one* all things in Christ, both which are in heaven and which are on earth." "To the intent that now unto the principalities and powers in heavenly places might be known by the Church the manifold wisdom of God, according to the eternal purpose which he purposed in Christ Jesus our Lord." Cherubim and seraphim stand unsandaled and uncovered in the presence of the glorious manifestations of the interior nature and essence of Deity, of the boundless wisdom and the love unfathomable displayed in the whole redemptive scheme: an immeasurable store of truth and life, illustrated in all the past, never to be exhausted in all the future.

To the young men who are present, ready to matriculate in this new seat of learning, who stand as the representatives of the great company of young men who, in the succession of generations, shall fill these ample halls, and be trained by the most eminent masters and instructors of the times in all learning, philosophy, and science, and go out to fill positions in society full of responsibility as well as honor—to you, allow me, before I sit down, a parting word.

It is this word of warning: Never to substitute *culture* for personal godliness. This is an error—may I venture to say *the* error, the fatal error—to which you will be most exposed on the intellectual side. No mere knowledge, even theological knowledge, can safely be put in the place of a personal regeneration brought into the spirit by the full, entire, unquestioning, irrevocable commitment of the soul to Jesus Christ as a Saviour. Knowledge will point out the path to this Saviour; a penitent faith, which has abandoned sin and broken with the world, walks in this path, and at the feet of the Son of God makes the actual, all-important surrender. This process never has been, never can be, superseded by mere education, since human nature has in itself no recuperative, self-reconstructive energies to be drawn out by culture. Our religion is the religion of *salvation;* and God's plan, which has settled the matter for all time, connects repentance toward God and faith toward our Lord Jesus Christ with salvation, as necessary conditions.

I know how strong are sometimes the excitements of the imagination; how liable we are to substitute these excitements in the place of a genuine faith in the Son of God. A refined taste may be quick to discern the sentiment of the beautiful in nature and art, in the breezy morn and the dewy eve, in mountain, and sky-glassing lake, and foaming water-fall—the sentiment of the sublime in the azure sky and rolling thunder, in the storm-swept sea, and under the midnight stars. It may linger along the haunts and drink at the fountain of the Muses—may be thrilled with the melting harmonies which swell through some grand old temple, or stand awed in the presence of smoking incense, white or scarlet robed processions, and priestly genuflections. Meanwhile, the conscience may never have weighed the imperatives which link the soul inextricably to a future retribution, the heart never have felt the bitterness of sin, the will never have accepted God's method of salvation, the spirit's free activities never have been turned to Christ as the only way to God.

But, with this word of warning, let me utter, also, the parting word of high, confident assurance, that Christ will bind into blessed agreement, bring into joyous accord, blend in beauteous symmetry, all that is truly valuable in the culture of intellect, in the play of sentiment and taste, all that is noble in secular learning, in philosophy and science, with all that is divine in a supernatural salvation, all that is deepest and loftiest in the knowledge and love of God. "By Him all things consist." "Put ye on the Lord Jesus, and make no provision for the flesh." Make a sincere surrender, an irrevocable commitment, to Him. Then, with an abiding consciousness that these are your own and real states of the mind, with "the peace of God, which passeth all understanding," keeping heart and mind, susceptibility and intellect, you will have the gates of the will guarded by sleepless sentinels. Infidel sophistry, false philosophy, the sneer and banter of a proud and daring scientism, the fury of an audacious criticism, denying the possibility of the supernatural, materializing the soul, grinding it to powder under the ponderous wheels of natural law, along with the body in death, and proclaiming annihilation as the goal of all aspiration—forces such as these, aided by the witchery of sensual pleasure, the waving plume, the painted cheek, the blazing diamond, the more lustrous eye of beauty, leading youth into the gas-lit halls of revelry—all these, and whatever else a state of trial for the unseen and eternal may allow or present, as antagonistic, and therefore as tests, to the faith of the Christian, you will be able to withstand, Christ being "in you the hope of glory." Or, if adversity befall, if health fail, if darkness come down, and great winds blow, and the vessel be tossed on a sea of tempests, over the troubled waves your faith shall see Him who of old, amid storm and darkness, said, "It is I, be not afraid!"

And, in fine, for all the possibilities, hazards, and hopes of the dread, sublime, "all-hail hereafter," Christ mani-

fested in the flesh, put to death under Pontius Pilate, risen from a sealed and guarded grave, ascended, invested with the "power of an endless life," behold the foundation of a hope that grasps the Infinite; see the tie between earth and heaven, between man and the eternal God.

May this great doctrine of Christ form the foundation-principle of every sermon and lecture which shall hereafter be delivered within these grand, echoing, and now consecrated, walls! To Him, the substance and supreme end of all preaching, of all culture, in all ages of time, to Him, "Jesus Christ, the same yesterday, to-day, and forever," be glory and dominion everlasting! "For thou only art the Lord; thou only, O Christ, with the Holy Ghost, art most high in the glory of God the Father."

The Dedication Ode (tune, Albion, or America) was sung, as follows:

Father Omnipotent,
Our offering we present,
  And trust thou wilt
Deign to accept what we,
With a glad heart and free,
Gratefully offer thee—
  Our Vanderbilt!

Incarnate Word Divine,
We offer thee this shrine,
  And trust thou wilt,
Great Sun of righteousness,
Beam forth with special grace,
And consecrate and bless
  Our Vanderbilt!

Creator Spirit, come,
And consecrate this dome!
  We trust thou wilt!
Descend from heaven above,
Like the symbolic dove,
And hover o'er, in love,
  Our Vanderbilt!

All-glorious One in Three,
This shrine we offer thee,
And know thou wilt,
For thy own mercy's sake,
In condescension take
The offering which we make—
Our Vanderbilt!

Prayer was offered by Dr. J. B. McFERRIN, followed by the Doxology:

To the great One and Three
Eternal praises be
Hence—evermore!
His sovereign majesty
May we in glory see,
And to eternity
Love and adore.

Bishop WIGHTMAN closed the service by pronouncing the Benediction.

ON Monday morning, October 4, at ten o'clock, under the escort of the Chief Marshal of the Day, His Excellency Governor PORTER, with the Bishops, Board of Trust, and Faculties, followed by the students, went in procession from the Chancellor's office to the Chapel.

After Music by the Band, a voluntary by the Choir, and Prayer by Bishop McTYEIRE, a splendid full-length portrait of Commodore VANDERBILT was unveiled, amid great applause.

The Governor was introduced by Bishop McTYEIRE, and His Excellency made a brief and pertinent Address, as follows:

Gentlemen of the Faculty, and Trustees of Vanderbilt University:

No event of its kind has awakened more of popular sympathy in the South, and especially in Tennessee, than the opening of this University. At the laying of the corner-stone of this magnificent building, my predecessor was here, and gave voice to the sentiments of his constituents; and I am here to-day to repeat the expression of satisfaction, common to the people of Tennessee, at the location of a great University at the capital of their State, and to extend to you, dignitaries of the Church—trustees, professors, and students—a cordial welcome to Tennessee; and I wish I could add a welcome to him who has given his name to the University, and whose munificence has given it life. His name must forever stand preëminent for its claim to a grateful recollection. His benevolence is superior to sections and to parties, and his liberality illustrates that character of men, common to our country, who raise trade and commerce above a mere selfish pursuit of individual gain.

The State offers to you no exclusive privileges, but it generously relieves your property from the ordinary burdens, and will afford to it the full protection of its laws. The Constitution of the State provides that "it shall be the duty of the General Assembly, in all future periods of this Government, to cherish literature and science." This provision in the fundamental law of the land is the warrant of the people of Tennessee that this institution shall have their protection and support.

Gentlemen, the mission of this University is above mere commonplace. It must be more than a place where academical instruction is imparted; it must be more than a school for the training of candidates for "the three learned professions." Steam and electricity are driving us forward at a tremendous pace, and, to meet the demands of the hour, you who are charged with the administration of this great trust, must, as I believe you will, make it a universal school, in which are taught all branches of learning: a *studium generale et Universitas studii generalis*, where architechts, chemists, engineers, farmers, and miners, can be ed ucated, and where original inquiries and investigations are stimulated. The duty assigned to me is simply to welcome you, Churchmen and school-men. I repeat my greeting, and bid you Godspeed.

After Music by the Band, the Rev. CHARLES F. DEEMS, D.D., delivered the following Address:

RELATIONS OF THE UNIVERSITY TO RELIGION.

Your Excellency, Mr. President of the Board of Trust, Mr. Chancellor, Gentlemen of the Faculties, Ladies and Gentlemen:

God, the Father of lights and of spirits, knows how profoundly I feel the responsibility of making the Opening Address of the VANDERBILT UNIVERSITY—an institution dear to me for many reasons, an institution which I hope will endure forever. Trusting in the God of nature and of grace, and resting on your friendly interpretation of all I shall say, I go forward.

Looking up, as in prayer, he said:

"Let the words of my mouth and the meditation of my heart be acceptable in thy sight, O Lord, my strength and my Redeemer."

It has been thought fit that a minister of religion should make the first utterances at the opening of a school which professes to intend to teach what is known, and to stimulate research, in every department of intellectual investigation. If, for a moment, any man could suppose that it would be proper to assign the initial speech to a teacher of religion as indicating that religion should take haughty and undue precedence of science, the thought would be most infelicitous. The present speaker would not assume any such position. It would misrepresent his convictions of the truth and his sense of the proprieties of the occasion.

This recent cry of the "Conflict of Religion and Science" is fallacious, and mischievous to the interests of both science and religion; and would be most mournful if we did not believe that, in the very nature of things, it must be ephemeral. Its genesis is to be traced to the weak foolishness of some professors of religion, and to the weak wickedness of some professors of science. No man of powerful and healthy mind, who is devout, ever has the slightest apprehension that any advancement of science can shake the foundations of that faith which is necessary to salvation. No man of powerful and healthy mind, engaged in observing, recording, and classifying facts, and in searching among them for those identities and differences which point to principles and indicate laws, ever feels that he suffers any embarrassment or limitations in his studies by the most reverent love he can have for God as his Father, or the most tender sympathy he can have for man as his brother, or that hatred for sin which produces penitence, or that constant leaning of his heart on God which produces spiritual-mindedness, or that hope of a state of immortal holiness which has been the ideal of humanity in all ages.

All this dust about "the conflict" has been flung up by men of insufficient faith, who doubted the basis of their faith; or by men of insufficient science, who have mistaken theology or the Church for religion; or by unreasonable and wicked men, who have sought to pervert the teachings of science so as to silence the voice of conscience in themselves, or put God out of their thoughts, so that a sense of his eternal recognition of the eternal difference between right and wrong might not overawe their spirits in the indulgence of the lust of the flesh, the lust of the eye, and the pride of life. It may be profitable to discriminate these; and if badges and flags have become mixed in this fray, it may be well to reädjust our ensigns, so that foes shall strike at only foes.

It is, first of all, necessary to settle distinctly what science is, as well as what it is not; and, also, what religion is, as well as what it is not.

We can all afford to agree upon the definition rendered by the only man who has been found in twenty-two centuries to add any thing important to the imperial science of logic. Sir William Hamilton defines science as "a complement of cognitions, having in point of form the character of logical perfection, and in point of matter the character of real truth." Under the focal heat of a definition like this, much that claims to be science will be consumed. It is the fashion to intimate, if not to assert, that it is much more easy to become scientific than to become religious; that in one case a man is dealing with the real, in the other with the ideal; in the one case with the comprehensible, in the other with the incomprehensible; in the one case with that which is certain and exact, and in the other case with that which at best is only probable and indefinite.

There can be no doubt, among thoughtful men, of the great value of both science and religion. A thinker who is worth listening to is always misunderstood if it be supposed that he means to disparage either. An attempt to determine the limits of religion is no disparagement thereof, because all the most religious men who are accustomed to think are engaged in striving to settle those limits, in order that they may have advantage of the whole territory of religion on the one hand, and on the other may not take that as belonging to religion which belongs to something else.

Now, if Sir William Hamilton's definition is to be taken, we shall perceive that he represents science in its quality, in its quantity, and in its form. Cognition of something is necessary for science. Then, (1) the knowledge of things known must be true; (2) that knowledge must be full, and (3) it must be accurate; it must be in such form as to be most readily and successfully used by the logical understanding for purposes of thought.

This sets aside very much that has been called science, and, as it seems, perhaps nearly all that which has been the material used by those who have raised the most smoke over this "conflict" question.

"Guesses at truth" are valuable only as the pecking at a plastered wall, to find where a wooden beam runs, is useful; but a guess is not knowledge. A working hypothesis would not be to be despised, although the student of science might feel quite sure in advance that when he had learned the truth in this department he would throw the hypothesis away. A working hypothesis, like a scaffold, is useful; but a scaffold is not a wall. Art is not science. Art deals with the appearances, science with the realities, of things. Art deals with the external, science with the internal, of a thing; art with the phenomenon, science with the *noumenon*. It must be the "*real* truth" which we know, and know truly.

Weak men on both sides have done much harm—the weak religionists by assuming, and the weak scientists by claiming, for guesses and hypotheses the high character and full value of real truth. The guesses of both have collided in the air, and a real battle seemed impending; but it was only "guesses" which exploded—bubbles, not bombs; and it is never to be forgotten that a professor of religion has just as much right to guess as a professor of science, and the latter no more right than the former, although he may have more skill.

No man can abandon a real truth without degradation to his intellectual and moral nature; but Galileo, Kepler, and Newton, in their studies from time to time, employed and discarded theory after theory, until they reached that which was capable of demonstration. It was only that which took its place as science. In the case of Kepler, it is known what great labor he spent in attempting to represent the orbit of Mars by combinations of uniform circular motion. His working hypothesis was the old doctrine of epicyclic curves. But his great labor was not fruitless, as has been carelessly asserted. The theory was false, and therefore not a part of real science; but, working on it, he discovered that the orbit of Mars is an ellipse, and this led him to the first of his three great laws of planetary motion, and enabled him almost immediately to discover the second. Here was a great intellect employing as a working hypothesis a theory which has always been false, and now is demonstrably false. It was not science.

Now if, while scientific men are employing working hypotheses merely as such, men representing religion fly at them as if they were holding those hypotheses as science, or if men representing science do set forth these hypotheses as if they were real knowledge of truth, and proceed to defend them as such, then much harm is done in all directions.

In the first instance, the religious man shows an impatience which is irreligious. "He that believeth doth not make haste." It is unfair to criticise any man while he is doing. Let him do what he will do; then criticise *the deed.* The artist has laid one pigment on his palette, and he is criticised before it is known what others he intends to mix with it, to procure what shade, to produce what effect. Wait until all the paint is on the canvas, and the artist has washed his brushes and drawn the curtain from his picture; then criticise *the picture.*

This impatient and weak criticism on the part of religious men is injurious to scientific progress, as well as to the progress of religion. For the latter, it makes the reputation of unfairness; for the former, it does one of two bad things:

it obstructs free discussion among students of science, or pushes them into a foolish defiance of religion. Men must co-work with those of their own sphere of intellectual labors. They must publish guesses, conjectures, hypotheses, theories. Whatever comes into any mind must be examined by many minds. It may be true, it may be false; there must be no prejudgment. Now if, because our scientific men are discussing a new view, our religious men fly among them and disturb them by crying "heresy," "infidelity," "atheism," those students must take time to repel the charges, and thus their work be hurt. If let alone, they may soon abandon their false theory. Certainly, if a proposition in science be false, the students of science are the men likeliest to detect the falsehood, however unlikely they may be to discover the truth that is in religion. Nothing more quickly destroys an error than to attempt to establish it scientifically.

The premature cries of the religious against the scientific have also the effect of keeping a scientific error longer alive. Through sheer obstinacy, the assailed will often hold a bad position, which, if not attacked, had been long ago abandoned. And we must have noticed that nature seems quite as able to make scientific men obstinate as grace to do this same work for the saints.

No man should be charged with being an atheist who does not, in distinct terms, announce himself to be such; and in that case the world will believe him to be too pitiful a person to be worth assailing with hard words. But as you may drive a man away from you by representing him as your enemy, so a scientific man may be driven from the Christian faith, if convinced that the Christian faith stands in the way of free investigation and free discussion; or, he may hold on to the faith because he has brains enough to see that one may be most highly scientific and most humbly devout at the same time; but by persecution he may be compelled to withdraw from open communion with "those who profess and call themselves Christians." Then both parties lose—what neither can well afford to lose—the respect and help which each could give the other. When the son of a religious teacher turns to the works of a man whom he has heard that father denounce, and finds in any one page of those books more high religious thought than in a hundred of his father's commonplace discourses, a sad state of feeling is produced, and many mistakes are likely to follow.

Sir William Hamilton's definition of science has for *genus* "a complement of cognitions," and for *differentia* "logical perfection of form," and "real truth of matter." The definition is a demand for a certain fullness. We can only conjecture, in the case of any particular science, how much knowledge such a man as Sir William Hamilton would regard as a "complement." But students of science do well to remind themselves that it is impossible to exceed, and very difficult to succeed, and the easiest thing imaginable to fall short. In other words, we have never been able to collect more material of knowledge than the plan of any temple of science could *work* in, and really did not demand for the completion of the structure, and that very few temples of science have been finished, even in the outline, while all the plain of thought is covered with ruins of buildings begun by thinkers, but unfinished for want of more knowledge. Even where there has been gathered a sufficient amount of knowledge to be wrought by the logical understanding into the form of a science, so that such a mind as Hamilton's would admit it as a science—*i. e.*, a sufficient complement of cognitions of truths put in logical form—another age of labor, in other departments, would so shrink this science that, in order to hold its rank, it would have to *work in* the matter of more knowledge, and, to preserve its symmetry, be compelled to reädjust its architectural outlines. In other words, what is science to one age may not be science to its successor, because that successor may perceive that, although its matter had the character of real truth, and its form the character of logical perfection, *as far as it went*, nevertheless, there were not enough cognitions; not enough, just because in the later age it was possible to obtain additional cognitions, which could not have been obtained earlier.

And, in point of fact, has not this been the history of each of the acknowledged sciences? And can any significance be assigned to Sir William Hamilton's definition without taking the word "complement" to mean *all the cognitions possible at the time?* Now, unless at one time men have more cognitions of any subject than at another time, one of two things must be true: either (1) no new phenomena will appear in that department, or (2) no abler observer will arise. But the history of the human mind in the past renders both suppositions highly improbable. If no new phenomena appear we shall have observers abler than have existed, because, although it were granted that no fresh accessions of intellectual power came to the race, each new generation of observers would have increased ability, because each would have the aid of the instruments and methods of all predecessors. When we go back to consider the immense labor performed by Kepler in his investigations which led to his brilliant discoveries, we feel that if his nerves had given way under his labors, and domestic troubles, and financial cares, or his industry had been just a little less tenacious, he would have failed in the prodigious calculations which led him to his brilliant discoveries, and gave science such a great propulsion. Just five years after the publication of Kepler's "New Astronomy" the Laird of

Merchison published, in Scotland, his "*Mirifici Logarithmorum Canonis Descriptio.*" If Kepler had only had Napier's logarithms! But succeeding students have enjoyed this wonderful instrumental aid, and done great mental work with less draught on their vital energies.

The very facts, then, which make us proud of modern science should make scientific men very humble. It will be noticed that the most arrogant cultivators of science are those who are most ready to assail such religious men as are rigid, and hold that nothing can be added to or taken away from theology; and such scientific men make this assault on the assumption that physical sciences are fixed, certain, and exact. How ridiculous they make themselves, a review of the history of any science for the last fifty years would show. Is there any department of physical science in which a text-book used a quarter of a century ago would now be put into the hands of any student? The fact is that any man, who is careful of his reputation, has some trepidation in issuing a volume on science, lest the day his publishers announce his book the morning papers announce, also, a discovery which knocks the bottom out of all his arguments. This shows the great intellectual activity of the age—a matter to rejoice in, but it should also promote humility, and repress egotism in all well-ordered minds. There is, probably, no one thing known in its properties and accidents, in its relations to all abstract truths and concrete existence. No one thing is exactly and thoroughly known by any man, or by all men. Mr. Herbert Spencer well says: "Much of what we call science is not exact, and some of it, as physiology, can never become exact." (Recent Discussions, p. 158.) He might have made the remark with greater width, and no less truth, since every day accumulates proof that that department of our knowledge which we call the exact sciences holds an increasingly small proportion to the whole domain of science.

There is one important truth which seems often ignored, and which should frequently be brought to our attention—viz.: that the propositions which embody our science are statements not of absolute truths, but of probabilities. Probabilities differ. There is that which is merely probable, and that which is more probable, and that which is still much more probable, and that which is so probable that our faculties cannot distinguish between this probability and absolute certainty; and so we act on it as if it were certain. But it is still only a "probability," and not a "certainty." It seems as though it would forever be impossible for us to determine how near a probability can approach a certainty without becoming identical with that certainty.

Is not all life a discipline of determining probabilities? It would seem that God intends that generally the certainties shall be known only to himself. He has probably shown us a very few certainties, more for the purpose of furnishing the idea than for any practical purpose, as absolute certainty is necessary for him, while probabilities are sufficient for us. All science is purely a classification of probabilities.

We do not *know* that the same result will follow the same act in its several repetitions, but *believe* that it will; and we believe it so firmly that if a professor had performed a successful experiment before a class in chemistry, he would not hesitate to repeat the experiment after a lapse of a quarter of a century. Scientific men are not infidels. Of no men may it be more truly said that they "walk by faith." They do not creep, they march. Their tread is on made ground, on probabilities; but they believe they shall be supported, and according to their faith so is it done unto them.

And no men better know than truly scientific men that this probability can never become certainty. In the wildest dreams of fanaticism—and there are fanatics in the laboratory, as there are in the sanctuary of God and in the temple of mammon—it has never been believed that there shall come a man who shall know all things that are, all things that have been, all things that shall be, and all things that can be, in their properties, their attributes, and their relations. Until such a man shall arise, science must always be concerned with the cognition of that which is the real truth as to probabilities, or with probable cognitions of that which is not only real truth, but absolute truth. A scientific writer, then, when he states that any proposition has been "proved," or any thing "shown," means that it has been proved probable to some minds, or shown to some—perhaps to all—intelligent persons as probable. If he have sense and modesty, he can mean no more, although he does not cumber his pages or his speech with the constant repetition of that which is to be presumed, even as a Christian in making his appointments does not always say, *Deo volente*, because it is understood that a Christian is a man always seeking to do what he thinks to be the will of God, in submission to the providence of God.

A scientific man ridicules the idea of any religious man claiming to be "orthodox." It must be admitted to be ridiculous, just as ridiculous as the claim of a scientific man to absolute certainty and unchangeableness for science. The more truly religious a man is, the more humble he is; the more he sees the deep things of God, the more he sees the shallow things of himself. He claims nothing positively. He certainly does not make that most arrogant of all claims, the claim to the prerogative of infinite intelligence. There can exist only one Being in the universe who is positively and absolutely orthodox, and that is God. In religion, as in science, we walk by faith—that is, we believe in the probabilities sufficiently to act upon them.

So far from any conflict being between science and religion, their bases are the same, their modes are similar, and their ends are identical—viz.: what all life seems to be, that is, a discipline of faith.

It is not proper to despise knowledge, however gained: whether from the exercise of the logical understanding, or from consciousness, or from faith; and these are the three sources of our knowledge. That which has been most undervalued is the chief of the three—that is, faith.

We *believe* before we acquire the habit of studying and analyzing our consciousnesses. We *believe* before we learn how to conduct the processes of our logical understanding.

We can have much knowledge by our faith without notice of our consciousness, and without exertion of our reasoning faculties; but we can have no knowledge without faith. We can learn nothing from our examination of any consciousness without faith in some principle of observation, comparison, and memory. We can acquire no knowledge by our logical understanding without faith in the laws of mental operations.

This last statement, if true, places all science on the same basis with religion. Although so familiar to many minds, we may take time to show that it is true.

For proof let us go to a science which is supposed to demonstrate all its propositions, and examine a student in geometry. We will not call him out on the immortal 47:I of Euclid. We can learn all we need from a bright boy who has been studying Euclid a week. The following may represent our colloquy:

"Q. Do you know how many right angles may be made by one straight line upon one side of another straight line?

"A. Yes; two, and only two. Innumerable angles may

be made by two straight lines so meeting, but the sum of all the possible angles will be two right angles.

"Q. You say you know that. How do you know that you know it?

"A. Because I can prove it. A man knows every proposition which he can demonstrate.

"Q. Please prove it to me."

The student draws the well-known diagrams. If he follows Euclid, he begins with an argument like this:

"A. There are obviously two angles made when a straight line stands on another straight line.

"Q. My eyes show me that.

"A. Well, then, those angles are either two right angles or, together, are equal to two right angles. And I prove that in this way: If the two angles made by the lines be equal, each is a right angle according to the definition of a right angle, which may be stated thus: A right angle is one of the two angles made by a straight line on one side of another straight line when both angles are equal. If each is a right angle, and there are only two, because they have taken all the space on that side of the line, it is proved that two right angles are made by two lines in the relation supposed, and only two."

But if each be not a right angle, our young friend proceeds, by the well-known demonstration of Euclid, to show that the sum of the two angles is equal to two right angles; and when he has finished and reached the Q. E. D., he and his examiners *know* that this proposition is true, because he has proved it. But when we examine his argument we find that he has made three unproved assumptions—namely, (1) that a thing cannot at the same time *be* and *not be;* (2) that if equals be added to equals the wholes are equal; and (3) that things which are equal to the same are equal to one another. It so happens that each of these propositions which he has assumed to be true is, if true, much more important than the proposition which he has proved. Let us point out these three assumptions to our bright student, and then resume our catechism.

"Q. Could you possibly prove this proposition in geometry if any one of those three assumed propositions were not granted?

"A. No.

"Q. Then, if we deny these assumptions, can you prove them?

"A. No; but can you deny them?

"No, we cannot deny them, and cannot prove them; but we believe them, and, therefore, have granted them to you for argument, and know your proposition of the two right angles to be true, because you have proved it."

Now, here is the proposition which Euclid selected as the simplest of all demonstrable theorems of geometry, in the demonstration of which the logical understanding of a student cannot take the first step without the aid of faith.

From the student let us go to the master. We go to such a teacher as Euclid, and in the beginning he requires us to believe three propositions, without which there can be no geometry, but which have never been proved, and, in the nature of things, it would seem never could be proved—namely, that space is infinite in extent, that space is infinitely divisible, and that space is infinitely continuous. And we believe them, and use that faith as knowledge, and no more distrust it than we do the results of our logical understandings, and are obliged to admit that geometry lays its broad foundations on our faith.

Now, geometry is the science which treats of forms in their relations in space. The value of such a science for intellectual culture and practical life must be indescribably important, as might be shown in a million of instances. No form can exist without boundaries, no boundaries without lines, no line without points. The beginning of geometric knowledge, then, lies in knowing what a "point" is, the existence of forms depending, it is said, upon the motion of points. The first utterance of geometry, therefore, must be a definition of a point. And here it is: "A point is that which has no parts, or which has no magnitude." At the threshold of this science we meet with a mystery. "A point is"—then, it has existence—"is" what? In fact, in form, in substance, it is nothing. A logical definition requires that the *genus* and *differentia* shall be given. What is the *genus* of a "point?" Position, of course. Its *differentia* is plainly seen. It is distinguished from every thing else in this, that every thing else is *something somewhere*, and a point is *nothing somewhere;* every thing HAS *some* characteristic, a point has *none*. A point is visible or invisible. Is it visible? Then, we can see that which is without parts or magnitude. What is it we see when we do not see any part, do not see any magnitude? Is it substantial or ideal? If substantial, how do we detect its substantial existence? If ideal, how can an idea have motion, and by simple motion become a substantial existence? Are we not reduced to this? Ideals produce substantials, or invisible substantials, upon motion, produce visible substantials; or that which is necessary to matter—namely, form—owes its existence to that which is neither substantial nor ideal—to nothing, in fact. The entire and sublime science of geometry, at one time the only instrument of culture among the Greeks, and so esteemed by Plato that he is said to have written over his door, "Let no one enter here who does not know geometry," in all its conceptions, propositions, and demonstrations, rests upon the conception of that which has no parts, no magnitude. The old saw of the school-men was, "*Ex nihilo nihil fit.*" If each visible solid owes its form to superficies, and each superficies its form to lines, and each line its form to a point—and a point has no form, because it has no parts—then, who shall stone the man that cries out, "*Ex nihilo geometria fit?*"

But lay the first three definitions of geometry side by side: 1. "A point is that which has no parts, or which has no magnitude." 2. "A line is length without breadth." 3. "The extremities of a line are points." Study these, and you will probably get the following results: That which has no parts produces all the parts of that which occupies space without occupying space, and which, although it occupies no space, has extremities, to the existence of which it owes its own existence; and those extremities determine the existence of that which has parts made up of multiplications of its extremities which have no parts. Now, you must know at least that much, or else stay out of Plato's house.

This useful science, without which men could not measure their little plantations, or construct their little roads on earth, much less traverse and triangulate the ample fields of the skies, lays for its necessary foundation thirty-five definitions, three postulates, and twelve axioms, the last being propositions which no man has ever proved; and these fifty sentences contain as much that is incomprehensible, as much that must be granted without being proved, as much that must be believed, although it cannot be proved, as can be found in all the theological and religious writings from those of John Scotus Erigina down to those of Richard Watson, of England, or Charles Hodge, of Princeton.

Does any man charge that this is a mere logical juggle? Then, he shall be called upon to point out wherein it differs from the methods of those who strive to show that there is a real conflict between real science and real religion. If any man shall charge me with being an infidel as touching geometry, and try to turn me out of the church of science, I shall become hotly indignant, because I know that Euclid did not believe more in geometry than I do, and I believe as much in the teachings of geometry as I do in the teachings of theology, regarding them both, as Aristotle did, as mere human sciences, ranking theology with psychology, geology, and botany. And, being by profession a theologian, I certainly believe in theology.

And this brings us back to what was stated in the beginning, as one of the causes of this cry of "conflict." It is the confounding of theology with religion. Theology is not religion any more than psychology is human life, or zoölogy is animal life, or botany is vegetable life. Theology is a human science; religion is a real life. Theology is objective; religion is subjective. Theology is the scientific classification of what is known of God; religion is a loving obedience to God's commandments. Every religious man must have some theology, but it does not follow that every theologian must have some religion. We never knew a religious man without some kind of a theology, nor can we conceive such a case. But we do know some theologians who have little religion, and some that seem to have none. There may be a conflict between theology and some other sciences, and religious men may deplore *that* conflict, or may not, according to their measure of faith. There are those whose faith is so large and strong that they do not deplore such a conflict, because they know that if, for instance, a conflict should come between geology and theology, and geology should be beaten, it will be so much the better for religion; and if geology should beat theology, still so much the better for religion: according to the spirit of the old Arabic adage, *If the pitcher fall on the stone, so much the worse for the pitcher; and if the stone fall on the pitcher, so much the worse for the pitcher.* Geologists, psychologists, and theologists, must all ultimately promote the cause of religion, because they must confirm one another's truths, and explode one another's errors; and a religious man is a man whose soul longs for the truth, who loves truth because he loves God, who knows if the soul be sanctified it must be sanctified by the truth, even as the mind must be enlarged and strengthened by the truth. He knows and feels that it would be as irreligious in him to reject any truth found in nature as it would be for another to reject any truth found in the Bible.

But there is no necessary conflict between even theology and any other science. Theology has to deal with problems into which the element of the infinite enters. It will therefore have concepts some two of which will be irreconcilable, but not therefore contradictory. For instance, to say that God is "an infinite person" is to state the agreement of two concepts which the human mind is supposed never to have reconciled, and never to be able to reconcile. But they are not contradictory. If one should say that there is in the universe a circular triangle, we should deny it, not because the concept of a triangle is *irreconcilable* with the concept of a circle, as consistent in the same figure, which is quite true, but because they are *contradictory.* What is irreconcilable to you may be reconcilable to another mind, because "irreconcilable" indicates the relation of the concept to the individual intellect; but what is contradictory to the feeblest is contradictory to the mightiest mind, because "contradictory" represents the relation of the concepts to one another.

In the definition of a *person* there is nothing to exclude infinity, and in the definition of *infinite* there is nothing to exclude personality. There is no more exclusion between "person" and "infinite" than between "line" and "infinite;" and yet we talk of infinite lines, knowing the irreconcilability of the ideas, but never regarding them as contradictory.

Writers of great ability sometimes fall into this indiscrimination. For instance, a writer whom I greatly admire, Dr. Hill, former President of Harvard College, in one paragraph (in "The Uses of Mathesis") seems twice to employ "contradictory" in an illogical sense, even when he is presenting an illustration which goes to show most clearly that in other sciences, as well as in theology, there are propositions which we cannot refuse to accept, because they are not contradictory, although they are irreconcilable; in other words, that there are irreconcilable concepts which are not contradictory, for we always reject one or the other of two contradictory concepts or propositions.

That is so striking an illustration of the mystery of the infinite that I will reproduce it. On a plane imagine a fixed line, pointing north and south. Intersect this at an angle of ninety degrees by another line, pointing east and west. Let this latter rotate at the point of intersection, and at the beginning be a foot long. At each approach of the rotating line toward the stationary line let the former double its length. Let each approach be made by bisecting the angle. At the first movement the angle would be forty-five degrees and the line two feet in length; at the second, the angle twenty-two and one-half degrees and the line four feet; at the third, the angle eleven and one-fourth degrees and the line eight feet; at the fourth, the angle five and five-eighths degrees and the line sixteen feet; at the fifth, the angle two and thirteen-sixteenths degrees and the line thirty-two feet, and so on. Now, as this bisecting of the angle can go on indefinitely before the rotating line can touch the stationary line at all its points, it follows that before such contact the rotating line will have a length which cannot be stated in figures, and which defies all human computation. It can be mathematically demonstrated that a line so rotating, and increasing its length in the inverse ratio of its angle with the meridian, will have its end always receding from the meridian and approaching a line parallel to the meridian at a distance of 1.5708. We can show that the rotating line can cross the stationary line by making it do so as on a watch-dial, and yet we can demonstrate that if it be extended indefinitely it can never touch the stationary line, nor come at the end even as near as eighteen inches to it.

Here are two of the simplest human conceptions, between which we know that there is no contradiction, rendered absolutely irreconcilable to the human intellect by the introduction of the infinite. There is no religion here. And yet there is no mystery in either theology or religion more mysterious than the mystery of the infinite, which we may encounter whenever we attempt to set our watches to the right time if they have run more than an hour wrong.

Another error has been the occasion of this cry of "conflict." It is the confounding of "the Church" with "religion." This confusion has led many an honest soul astray, and is the fallacy wherewith shrewd sophists have been able to overthrow the faith of the ignorant. If the Church—and, in all my treatment of this topic, I must be understood as using "the Church" not as signifying "the holy Church universal," but simply in the sense in which antagonistic scientists employ it—if *the Church* and *religion* be the same, the whole argument must be given up, and it must be admitted that there is a conflict between religion and science, and that religion is in the wrong. Churchmen are guilty of helping to strengthen, if indeed they are not responsible for creating, this error. It has at length been presented plumply to the world in the book of Professor John William Draper, entitled a "History of the Conflict between Religion and Science." The title assumes that there is such a conflict. See how it will read with synonyms substituted: "History of the Conflict between *Loving Obedience to God's Word* and *Intelligent Study of God's Works.*" Does Dr. Draper believe there is such a conflict? It is not to be supposed that he does. How, then, did he come to give his book such a title? From a confusion of terms, as will be observed by the perusal of three successive sentences in his preface: "The *papacy* represents the ideas and aspirations of two-thirds of the population of Europe. It insists on a political supremacy, ... loudly declaring that it will accept no reconciliation with modern civilization. The antagonism we *thus* witness between *religion* and science," etc. Now, if "the papacy" and "religion" be synonymous terms, representing equivalent ideas, Dr. Draper's book shows that all good men should do what they can to extirpate religion from the world; but if they are not—and they are not—then the book is founded on a most hurtful fallacy, and must be widely mischievous. Their share of the responsibility for the harm done must fall to Churchmen.

No, these are not synonymous terms. "The Church" is *not* religion, and religion is *not* "the Church." There may be a Church and no religion; there may be religion and no Church, as there may be an aqueduct without water, and there be water without an aqueduct. God makes water, and men make aqueducts. Water was before aqueducts, and religion before Churches. God makes religion, and men make Churches. There are irreligious men in every Church, and there are very religious men in no Church. Any visible, organized Church is a mere human institution. It is useful for the purpose of propagating religion so long as it confines itself to that function and abstains from all other things. The moment it transcends that limit, it is an injurious institution. In either case it is merely human, and we wrong both religion and the Church when we claim for the latter that it is not a human institution. The Church of England is as much a human institution as the Royal Society; and the same may be said of the Church of Rome and the Royal Florentine Academy. A Church is as much an authority in matters of religion as a society is in matters of science, and no more. "The Church" has often been opposed to science, and so it has to religion; but "the society" has often been opposed to religion, and so it has to science. "The Church," both before and since the days of Christ, has stood in opposition to the Bible, the text-book of Jewish and Christian religionists, quite as often as it has to science. But "the society," or "the academy," has stood in opposition to science quite as often as it has to religion. Sometimes the sin of one has been laid upon the other, and sometimes the property of one has been scheduled as the assets of the other. It is time to protest, in the interests of the truth of God, and in the name of the God of truth, that religion no longer be saddled with all the faults of the Churchmen, all the follies of the scientists, and all the crimes of the politicians. It was not religion which brought Galileo to his humiliating retraction, about which we hear so much declamation; it was "the Church."

But why should writers of the history of science so frequently conceal the fact that "the Church" was instigated thereunto not by religious people, but scientific men—by Galileo's *collaborateurs?* It was the jealousy of the scientists which made use of the bigotry of the Churchmen to degrade a rival in science. They began their attacks not on the ground that religion was in danger, but on such scientific grounds as these, stated by a professor in the University of Padua—namely, that as there were only seven metals, and seven days in the week, and seven apertures in man's head, there could be only seven planets! And that was some time before these gentlemen of science had instigated the sarcastic Dominican monk to attempt to preach Galileo down under the text, *Viri Galilœi, quid statis adspicientes in cœlum?*

In like manner, politicians have used "the Church" to overthrow their rivals. "The Church" is the engine which has been turned against freedom, against science, against religion. It would be as logical and as fair to lay all "the Church's" outrages against human rights and intellectual advancement at the door of religion as it would be to lay all its outrages against religion at the door of science and government, because "the Church" has seldom slaughtered a holy martyr to the truth without employing some forms of both law and logic.

Science exists for the sake of religion, and because of religion. If there had been no love for God in the human race, there had been no study of the physical universe. The visible cosmos is God's love-letter to man, and religion seeks to probe every corner of the sheet on which such love is written, to examine every phrase, and study every connection. A few upstarts of the present day, not the real men and masters of science, ignore the fact that almost every man who has made any great original contribution to science, since the revival of letters, was a very religious man; but their weak wickedness must not be charged to science any more than the wicked weakness of ecclesiastics to religion.

Copernicus (born 1473), who revolutionized astronomy, was one of the purest Christians who ever lived—a simple, laborious minister of religion, walking beneficently among the poor by day, and living among the stars by night; and yet one writer of our day has dared to say, in what he takes to be the interest of science, that Copernicus was "aware that his doctrines were totally opposed to revealed truth."

Was any thing worse ever perpetrated by theologian, or even ecclesiastic? Could *any* man believe in any doctrine which he *knew* was opposed to any truth, especially if he believed that God had revealed that truth? It were impossible, especially with a man having the splendid intellect and the pure heart of Copernicus, who died believing in his "*De Orbium Cœlestium Revolutionibus*," and also in the Bible. And this is the inscription which that humble Christian ordered for his tomb: "*Non parem Paulo veniam requiro, gratiam Petri neque posco; sed quam in crucis ligno dederis latroni, sedulus oro.*"

Tycho Brahe (born 1546), who, although he did not produce a system which won acceptance, did, nevertheless, lay the foundation for practical astronomy, and build the stairs on which Kepler mounted to his grand discoveries, was a most religious man. He introduces into one of his scientific works ("*Astronomiæ Instauratio Mechanica*," p. A) this sentence: "No man can be made happy, and enjoy immortal life, but through the merits of Christ, the Redeemer, the Son of God, and by the study of his doctrines, and imitation of his example."

John Kepler (born 1571) was a man in whose life the only conflict between science and religion seemed to be as to which should yield the most assistance to the other. He wrought as under Luther's motto, "*Orasse est studisse.*" He prayed before he worked, and shouted afterward. The more he bowed his soul in prayer, the higher his intellect rose in its discoveries; and as those discoveries thickened on his head, it bowed in humbler adoration. And so that single man was able to do more for science than all the irreligious scientists of the last three centuries have accomplished, while he bore an appalling load of suffering with a patience that was sublime, and, dying, left this epitaph for his tomb-stone: "*In Christo pie obiit.*"

Of Sir Isaac Newton's, and Michael Faraday's, and Sir William Hamilton's, and Sir James Y. Simpson's religious life, not to mention the whole cloud of witnesses, we need not tell what is known to all men. But the history of science shows that not the most gifted, not the most learned, not the most industrious, gain the loftiest vision, but that only the pure in heart see God. And all true science is a new sight of God.

Herbert Spencer says: "Science may be called an extension of the perceptions by means of reasoning." (Recent Discussions, p. 60.) And we may add, Religion may be called an extension of the perceptions by means of faith. And having so said, have we not paraphrased Paul? "Faith is confidence in things hoped for, conviction of things not seen." (Heb. xi. 1.) Science has the finite for its domain, religion the infinite; science deals with the things seen, and religion with the things not seen. When Dr. Hutton, of Edinburgh, announced, in the last century, "In the economy of the world I can find no traces of a beginning, no prospect of an end," it is said that scientific men were startled and religious men were shocked. Why should they be? The creation of the universe and its end are not questions of science, and can be known only as revealed to faith. And so Paul says: "Through faith we apprehend intellectually that the worlds have been framed by the word of God, so that that which is seen may have sprung from that which is not seen." (Heb. xi. 3.)

But we must close.

While preparing this Address it has been my almost daily custom to pass the massive Masonic Temple recently erected in the city of New York. Before its portals stand two stately columns, known to the brethren of the Masonic Order as Jachin and Boaz. On each rests a globe. In going to my study in the morning I pass first the column which supports the celestial globe, and as I return to my home in the evening I pass first the column which supports the terrestrial globe. One day it came to me that here there stood, in solid symmetry and solemn resemblance, the symbols of these twins of God, who did not struggle in the infinite womb as Isaac's sons contended before they were born, and whose children should not fight on the fields of the finite as the descendants of Jacob and Esau have contended for inheritances which are corruptible and which pass away.

The most sacred thing in the "*Sanctum Sanctorum*" of the ancient Hebrew tabernacle and temple was the Ark of the Covenant, the Law, God's testimony to his sense of right, the solitary autograph in human letters of the Eternal, written on stone, inscribed by the very fingers of the Lord God Almighty. Over the Ark which held the Law, God ordered that a Mercy-seat should be placed. "His tender mercies are over all his works," and so his Mercy-seat covered his Testimony. When Adam and Eve had been driven forth, the cherubim had stood at Eden's gate, while a flaming sword turned every way. They were placed there as guardians to keep the way of the tree of life. In the tabernacle the cherubim reäppear, but come without the sword, stretching forth their wings on high, covering the Mercy-seat with their wings, and gazing down on the awful mystery of Love overlapping Law, and Law upholding Love.

Behold, I have a vision of the cherubim.

The Ark is carried into the temple not made with hands, eternal in the heavens. The cherubim are instinct with life to the outermost tip of each mighty pinion. The very glory of God descends to make his everlasting throne upon the everlasting Mercy-seat, which covers the everlasting Seat of Law. Before the infinite majesty of that Glory the cherubim arise, and stand in front of God; and, as they arise, the sounds of their quivering wings are heard to the outer court of all the temple of the universe, as the voice of the Almighty God when he speaketh.

See how they stand, so vast and so superb!

The One who has the place by the right hand of the Omnipotent lifts up himself, and all the glory of all the suns is on his brow, and each great wing is like an unmeasured milky-way, ashimmer with the mystic splendor of all stars.

The One who has the place nearest the infinite heart of Immortal Love lifts up himself. His brow is fairer than the light of that morning when all the sons of God shouted for joy. His eyes are lovelier than the sapphired tent that pavilions the eternal throne. His lips are ravishingly sweet with the best beauty that comes from the kisses of the Lord. His wings are pinions whose plumes of whiteness shed thoughts of purity down on angelic minds, and whose immense sweep fans all the love-flames glowing in seraphic hearts.

Twain they stand, and twain they turn, until hierarchic circles kindle into rapture at the sight. Even God delights himself in their surpassing glory, and smiles upon them until their vast hearts can no longer hold their divinest joy.

Twain they sing. The cherub of the snow-white wings and palpitating heart breaks heaven's ecstatic silence with the chant, "Holy, Holy, Holy, Lord God of Hosts!"

The cherub of the starry wings and throbbing brain gives antiphone, "Heaven and earth are full of the majesty of thy glory."

The heavens can keep silence no more, but seraphim and cherubim, angels and archangels, shout, shout up at the throne of Love and Law, "Glory be to thee, O Lord Most High!" and, from the farthest reach of thought and feeling, all the company of heaven fill the temple of God with the multitudinous and musical thunder of the united and overwhelming, "Amen, and Amen!"

And the King, eternal, immortal, invisible, the only wise God our Saviour, wraps those interlocked cherubim in his loving arms, and thrills the heavens with his royal edict, "What God hath joined together let not man put asunder."

Those cherubim sublime are science and religion. As they had no struggle with each other when God gave them birth, as they had no conflict guarding the Ark of Law and Love, as they shall have no discord when leading the choirs of eternity, so they have no conflict now. At the opening of this great University, heaven and earth unite in saying, "If any man in these halls shall ever teach that there is real conflict between real science and real religion, let that man be *Anathema Maranatha.*"

Pausing a moment at the close of his Address, Dr. DEEMS turned to Governor PORTER, and said:

YOUR EXCELLENCY:—Our friend, whose name this Institution bears, has communicated with you by letter, expressing his appreciation of your Excellency's courtesy in giving the emphasis of your official solicitation to the consideration extended him by the municipal authorities of Nashville, in the expression of their desire to make him the city's guest during these festive days of the inauguration of the University.

He did me the honor to request me to bring to your Excellency his respectful salutations, and to assure you that good and sufficient reasons exist for his absence, which is due to no lack of interest in this great Commonwealth of Tennessee, nor in this good city of Nashville, nor in this young University, for which he has done what he has done trusting that it will promote the general interests of learning, and of this whole nation, without regard to sect or section. [Applause.]

I have taken this occasion to make to you, publicly, a communication which might have been rendered in private had fitting opportunity occurred.

Since I came to my place in this Chapel, sir, a telegram has been handed me, which I shall take the liberty of reading to the whole audience.

The speaker then took from the desk an envelope, which he opened, and read the following telegram:

NEW YORK, Oct. 4.—To Dr. CHARLES F. DEEMS: Peace and good-will to all men. C. VANDERBILT.

This evoked hearty and prolonged applause from the audience.

Gazing a few moments on the portrait of Commodore VANDERBILT, which hung on the wall to his left, Dr. DEEMS, with great tenderness of feeling, quoted the passage of Holy Scripture (Acts x. 31):

CORNELIUS, thy prayer is heard, and thine alms are had in remembrance in the sight of God.

The eyes of the audience having been turned to the Commodore's portrait, this remark of Dr. DEEMS kindled a degree of enthusiasm that found vent in an emphatic outburst of approval. The scene was one of a highly impressive and even dramatic force.

After more Music, the Rev. A. A. LIPSCOMB, D.D., late Chancellor of the University of Georgia, delivered the following Address:

RELATIONS OF THE UNIVERSITY TO GENERAL EDUCATION.

LADIES AND GENTLEMEN:—Great ideas, like great men, are capable of unlimited growth. This is the inborn sign of their prerogative, this the outward seal of their sovereignty, that they are full of instructive life; so that one may describe them as Milton his angels—"vital in every part." Whether you take them in their sterner logic, or in their gentler sentiment, they expand with steady aim toward those ideals in which they are consummated. "*Be ye therefore perfect,*" is God's command to every grand truth; and the edict is sure of obedience. Like John the Baptist, they may go into the wilderness, but as the "*locusts and wild honey*" nourished his strength and courage, so they find even in dreary solitudes the means of constant nurture. Whatever the eagle feeds on turns to eagle; and so, too, no matter what may be the nutriment of great ideas, they are certain to rise into loftier proportions and reach forth into broader compass. Nay, more: the very souls into which they enter, conscious of a supreme power to vitalize every thing they embrace, breathe into them a new vigor; and thus from within no less than from without these truths press forward to their destiny. For in this faith we must abide, that every fact involving the well-being of our race has somewhere in its keeping the blessed Christ of humanity; and only give it time and opportunity, and the Infinite Presence will make itself known.

But "time and opportunity" are not always words of the same meaning. It pleases God at certain seasons to accelerate the movements of human society, to enhance rapidly the development of great ideas, and compress ages into a day. The electricity may gather slowly, but the lightning flashes quickly. So, then, we must take account of impulse as well as of uniform law, remembering that Jehovah "*maketh the clouds his chariot,*" and "*walketh upon the wings of the wind.*" Between the Hebrew of the Judges and the Hebrew of the monarchy only a small space lay, and yet what a moral reach of intervening years! From the Greece of

Herodotus, who stood in the transfiguring glories of her Marathon and Platææ, to the Greece of Thucydides, in the sunset of her Periclean age—only three-fourths of a century—what mighty periods and marvelous transitions interpose! Rome, too, was many Romes from the career of the Gracchi to the fall of Antony and Cleopatra. Nearer home, from Elizabeth to Cromwell, what an England sprang into power by means of domestic parties and foreign policy! Still nearer, if you look at that phase of American civilization which began with George Washington and ended with Robert E. Lee, how significant the series of amazements! To prevent men's minds from hardening under the monotony of law, it sometimes happens that Providence imparts a sudden momentum to moral and spiritual agencies; and thus we learn to wonder while we adore, and acquire, at the same time, a rational distrust of those mechanical sequences which, to a careless eye, seem to govern the social world.

Our day and our continent afford many typical illustrations of the force of great truths—of their prodigious vitality, of their steady expansion, and, moreover, of those quickening vivifications to which allusion has been made. The new world we inhabit under the skies of the West has lost most of its aborigines, and many of its close forests, and much of the old look of the landscapes; yet it is a newer world than when Plymouth Rock and Jamestown first received their immortal names. Recent astronomy has vastly enlarged our conception of the universe, but what shall we say of the widening out in all directions of the sphere of modern life? How the ancient Methuselah felt—patriarch of patriarchs, nine centuries gathered moment by moment into his heart—how he felt in that early Asia, none can imagine; but if our great-grandfathers could return to this land, we can easily conceive what changes would most fascinate their eyes. Franklin and Bowditch; the old minister Maury, who sketched for the boy Jefferson, three generations ago, the water-courses beyond the Rocky Mountains; Lewis and Clarke; later still, Fulton and Whitney—these men would see the magnitude of physical transformations that have gone on, partly by regular growth and partly by violent convulsion, since they left the earth. Nothing, however, would touch them so deeply as the progress of mind by means of education, and especially that aspect of education in which we gain a clear comprehension of the providential law under which man is ordained to recover the lost sovereignty over nature. This is, indeed, the foremost wonder of the times, since all other wonders are but its offspring.

Among the growths, then, of the century, we are warranted in putting a marked emphasis on the enlargement of the idea of education. You are the witnesses how wondrously it has developed. Look at the range of subjects taught, and you feel the force of a remark made to me by a learned friend, a graduate of fifty years since, that the science of chemistry now covers more ground than all the sciences covered together when he was a student in college. Look at the co-relations of the arts and sciences—their mutuality of action and interaction, their potent interchanges of impulse and influence, and their singular convergence in the same predestined ends! Look at the aid that philosophy has rendered to history and criticism, and the invaluable service that mental physiology has afforded to metaphysics! Classify your schools—the common, the academic, the industrial, the scientific—those for arts and those for professions, and follow them out in the work they do and the way they do it, and learn something of the area of modern education. Turn your eye to Bell and Lancaster, to Pestalozzi, to John Pounds, the poor shoemaker, with his ragged boys, to the genius of Seguin, in his "Idiot School," and then to the universities that send forth Pitt and Burke, Macaulay and Gladstone, ready-made, to enter on a national arena and bring instant help to their country. Passing from this survey, consider more carefully the introduction of a clearer and broader philosophy into the art of instruction—the improvement in modes and methods, the enlarged scope of relations between teachers and students, and the increased proportion of educated minds under these recent systems of education—and this growth will be still more obvious. Can you not discern these "*signs of the times?*" The extremes of utilitarianism and esthetics, of monarchy and democracy, of Church and State, have met here in the unanimity of generous enthusiasm.

Bear in mind, then, that it is not merely, or even mainly, in the extension of art and science we are to study the growth of education. The sentiment itself is quite different from the materials on which it works, and the products it creates. As a sentiment, education had at first a narrow range. Its advantages, such as they were, belonged to a few. Castes and classes afterward shared its patrimony. In part by its own inherent force, in part because of political and social revolutions, its domain has enlarged. Whether we go back to the invention of printing, or to the rise of Methodism, or to the effects of the French Revolution, one thing is clear, that the idea of education has been outreaching its former limitations, and finding "fresh woods and pastures new." To-day its stronghold is the education of the community, the nation, the race. And it shows its divine power in this, that it was once and so long "*a little leaven;*" for had it not been so "*little,*" it could never have permeated the bulky whole. Nor should we forget that the perfection of education, viewed as a sentiment, cannot be reached until we share its benefits with others. One of the many points at which true culture blends with true religion is in fulfilling the words, "*It is more blessed to give than to receive;*" while it is equally certain that the grandest thoughts lose their inspiration and fall back dead upon the heart unless we impart them to the world. A student of astronomy has much to learn beyond the boundary which Sir Isaac Newton touched. The pupil Faraday outstripped, by many brilliant leagues of space, his great teacher, Sir Humphrey Davy. But when we congratulate ourselves on the advance of knowledge, let us remember, too, as a ground of devout thanksgiving, that the recipients of the blessings of education embrace all orders and gradations of society. I consider no festival of scholars complete without the presence of this joy. And on a day like this, when we celebrate the advent of a new university, let it give a richer melody to our anthems of praise, that the idiot boy is now emancipated from the tyrannic bondage of the body; that the little children exchange their mothers' arms for the tender companionships of the kindergarten; that industrial schools extend a helping hand to the sons and daughters of the unhappy poor; and that all classes of people, from the humblest to the highest, are strengthened, cheered, ennobled, by those varied agencies of beneficence which modern education includes.

Looking at the historic development of education, we see that the few have given intellectual guidance and impulse to the many; or, in other words, the universities have been the fountain-heads whence have issued the streams of knowledge. For a long period the ancient universities of Oxford, Cambridge, Paris, Salamanca, and Bologna, were the only centers of instruction in Europe. These antedated by centuries the great school systems which are now acting on the masses. But for Oxford and Cambridge, Christ's Hospital, and Rugby, and Winchester, would not have been known.

About the year 1800 Humboldt presented to the King of Prussia the scheme of the Royal University of Berlin, and out of that have come the gymnasia which have done so much for that kingdom. Had not Harvard and Yale been early founded in the colonization of this country, the common schools of New England could not have sprung so soon into existence. To this rule there seem to be no valid exceptions. Mountains supply fertility to valleys; rivers that measure continents have sources lofty and remote; clouds may gather over this or that section of the globe, but they owe their waters to the immense oceans; and just so the higher universities have sent down their fertilizing power into every department of learning. This has not been an accident. It is one of the oldest and grandest of those laws by which the Eternal Wisdom has assured the world of its sovereign presence. Sometimes one man, at other times several men—single stars or constellations of splendor in the firmament—the few leading the many; so has it ever been as far back as we can penetrate. Out of Abraham, the elect Hebrew nation; out of Moses, all legislators; out of Homer, the culture of Greece; out of Julius Cesar, Augustus and the Empire. And how strikingly the Lord Jesus exemplified this divine method! Twelve men were taught and trained to spread Christianity throughout the world. In these chosen apostles, each fitted for his special task, Samaria, Syria, Asia Minor, Italy, lay imbedded for future development.

But a general statement is not enough. If we descend to particulars, we find that the best text-books in all departments of instruction, the progress made in the science of teaching whereby such an advance has been effected in the methods of acquisition and creation, the growing dignity of the teacher's office, have all proceeded from that kind of thought, and those modes of research, and preëminently from that philosophy of mind, which it is the function of the university to foster. More than this, the university devotes itself to those abstruse investigations, common alike to mind and matter, which are essential as the foundations of practical knowledge. A world without abstract truths, without the profundity of logic, without the subtle analyses of metaphysics, without the rules and *formulæ* of rigid science, could not be the world of either student or scholar; nor, indeed, could it be, in any significant sense, the world of political economy, or government, or trade and commerce. On the one hand, then, the simple match that lights your fire; the cooking-stove which educates your servant in a thoughtfulness and skill impossible in an open fire-place; higher far in the scale, chloroform and other anæsthetic agents, that conquer pain in the hiding-places of the nerves; and yet, again, those applications of mechanics which have made the earth so much worthier a habitation and a home for man—none of these things, in their varying degrees of utility and beneficence, could ever have been known except for that higher science which has its seat of authority and its scope of original action in the university.

On the other hand, take those books that are libraries in themselves. Call over such works as Butler's "Analogy," Paley's "Evidences," Blackstone's "Commentaries," Milton's "Paradise Lost," Adam Smith's "Political Economy," Bridgewater's "Treatises," Ranke's "History," and Humboldt's "Cosmos," and show me how these could have been possible but for that maturity of intellect and vastness of erudition which the university encourages and sustains. When, therefore, you think of the relations of the university to general education, recall the names of the Herschels, of Cuvier and Owen, of Dugald Stewart and Sir William Hamilton, of Black and Liebig, of Carpenter and Müller, of Neander and Chalmers, and in the light of their labors estimate the worth of this rarer culture. The standards of intellectual excellence which these men set themselves to attain were not self-originated, nor, indeed, can we affirm that their efforts were altogether self-directed. All unawares to themselves, and in entire accord with their personality, the spirit of university-culture shaped their minds and pursuits, and insensibly made them what they were in science and literature. Think, too, of Luther, and the indebtedness of the Reformation to the university. And think, likewise, of Wesley, and bless the providence that, amid its other signs of grace, ordained the birth-place of Methodism beneath the overshadowing centuries of Oxford University.

Having thus noticed the relations of the university to general education, I pause a moment to say that the attitude of the university is one of deep interest. Unquestionably, it is a formative force, a supreme force, in the world of mind. The more truthful its ideal, the higher will be that ideal. Men cannot outgrow its guidance and help. Men will be educated and ennobled just in the proportion that they reverence its spirit.

By virtue, therefore, of its position and accredited claims, the university has an authority peculiar to itself. Among us this authority rests on grounds intellectual and moral, and exerts itself in an influence subtle and pervasive. Without the appliances of secular power, it has a certain sovereignty which acts on public opinion, and still more on public sentiment. Although it cannot be measured by a palpable standard, it is none the less operative and controlling. Its very quality, so silent and unobtrusive, determines its commanding force; and for this reason its responsibilities, both as to the limits of its sphere and the duties within that sphere, are momentous. Only in the realization of its solemn trust, only in the profound feeling that it is a providential agency, called and commissioned for a great work, can the university find the sustenance of its strength and activity. It must be free from that worldliness which tremulously consults the tastes of a fugitive hour, panders to inconsiderate caprices, and bribes patronage into its support. Its creed cannot be taken from the exchange, nor its code from the street. The moment it undertakes to do its business after the manner of trade and commerce, its heart dies. It must be independent; it must stand above noisy clamor and passionate criticism; it must call no man master; but in the spirit of noblest manliness—calm, self-poised, and bravely earnest—it must obey the law of its vocation.

Standing, then, in this attitude, the university is bound, in duty, to recognize every department of true thought, every branch of genuine knowledge, every mode of thorough culture, and, moreover, to give each and all its sympathy, its support, its furtherance. It owes this to itself, to its historic antecedents, to the cause of education. Narrowness, overloaded bias, chronic prejudices, are fatal to its aims. One-sided universities make one-sided men, and one-sided men are never honest students nor reliable scholars. A true university has no pets, no hobbies. Holding itself sternly aloof from the partisanships which writhe the age into all sorts of distortions, it must be "dowered with the scorn of scorn and hate of hate," and press closely to its heart this truth, that Pharisaism is as deadly in science and art as in religion; its deadliness lying in this, that it is dogmatic, exclusive, denunciatory. The fault in all our thinking is want of breadth. A bird may sing in its confining cage, a lion be a lion behind his imprisoning bars, but a man shut up in pettiness and conceits is a fractional creature. What is best in the university is the catholicity of its views. Far more than its scope of technical inquiry, or its contributions to the world's stock of knowledge, is that majestic vigor of mind which has no taint of selfishness, which lives on disinterested service as its daily bread from heaven, which "looks before and after," and which, not content to go

> Round the daily scene
> Of sad subjection and of sick routine,

is ever striving to widen the reach of its horizon, and ever longing to see its zenith rise to a height more distant and more effulgent.

The infinite wisdom and power of Christianity cannot be embodied at present in any one Church. There are, consequently, many Churches, each sharing in that glory which is ineffable. The compass of humanity is too big to be limited in one nationality, and hence the variety of nations. Just so, education is a vast idea, needing many forms to give it shape and accommodate its substance. Chief of these is the university. Because of this superiority, its excellence mainly dwells in its broad and generous sentiment. Not otherwise can it be in coalescence with civilization and Christianity. Against what is local and sectional, against what is spasmodic and romantic, against every thing even tinged with self-idolatry, it must resolutely set itself, and take its stand on whatever is large-minded and enduring. It will never flatter the present at the expense of the past; still less will it be mean enough to thank God that it is "*not as other men are.*" Fraternity with all schools and colleges; sympathy with the proper work of the press, the bar, the medical profession, and the pulpit; heartiness of accord with the mechanic, the agriculturist, the navigator, the engineer, the manufacturer, and the merchant—these are the attestations of its office. Actuated, yea, inspired, by this sentiment, it will make itself felt in mines, and foundries, and workshops, in the cottages of the poor, and the mansions of the rich. For immediate results, it will walk abreast with the age; for yet grander results, it will transcend the age. But, in its diversified activity, it will keep paramount a simple unity of purpose; nor will it ever forget that its electness of ministration consists in binding together as one "*whatsoever things are true, whatsoever things are honest, whatsoever things are just, whatsoever things are pure, whatsoever things are lovely, whatsoever things are of good report.*"

Too much stress can scarcely be laid on the point now under consideration. As we ascend in the scale of education, we approach nearer to the moral and spiritual nature of man. At every step of progress manhood is more and more a vital issue. Culture is not religion; no matter how complete and beautiful, it is culture, and nothing else. Nevertheless, as it advances, it increases its capacity to assimilate with Christian virtue and be absorbed in its incomparably higher excellence. Now, in this respect, the university can accomplish much for learning and piety by the spirit animating its efforts. If selfishness of intellect is here engendered, if a cold and carping criticism is encouraged, if the disguises and deceits of bigotry are allowed, the effect is inevitably hurtful to both education and religion. Is it nothing to display an open-handed hospitality to all truth? Is it nothing to mediate between antagonistic elements, to reconcile hostile forces, to draw men together in the unity of a scholarly temper, and in the bonds of intellectual brotherliness? Is it nothing to promote humility of judgment? Is it not, indeed, a great thing to feel that somewhat of the mind of St. Paul may be ours, when, in the consciousness of his manifold gifts, he declared that he was a debtor to all mankind?

Indirectly, then, as well as directly, the university may

stimulate men to the practice of that "*charity*" which, in the realm of learning no less than in the realm of Christianity, is the "*greatest*." It can help men to be brethren. In our day, what humiliating conflicts between men of letters are going on! No one supposes that these struggles of opinion can be arrested; but the bitterness of the strife might be ended, for a debate need not be a duel. Right here the university has an open door of usefulness; for it is not what this or that branch of knowledge is in itself, nor what the professions or industrial interests are in themselves, but what they are united as auxiliaries to the growth of society and to the completeness of manhood, that decides their ultimate value. By appreciating this inter-relationship of all intellectual activities, and blending them in fellowship, the university may assume the leadership of mind. To combine, as far as practicable, the working brain, and the working heart, and the working hand, of this disjointed world is one of the worthiest of achievements. It is mediation, and therefore godlike. The human heart has been sadly dissevered from intellect, so that our truest organ of vision has been well-nigh lost; but this spirit restores it to its rightful place in the university. Men cannot love the truth and not love humanity. If this genial sympathy rule the university, one of the effects will be the education of well-bred intellects. Such minds are always rare. A thoroughly well-bred intellect is the perfection of good-breeding; and the university ought to make sure, at least, of this admirable product. An intellectual bully is the extreme of scholarly degradation; but is this odious sight uncommon in our time? Delicate refinement in unison with sturdy vigor, tenderness lending its grace to heroism, noble magnanimity side by side with unswerving integrity, truthfulness compact like a rock, and beauty garlanding the bare massiveness —these are the authentic seals of university work. In promoting this unity of culture, the university arrays itself against all sectionalism; it encourages internationality, and widens one's country beyond its shores. Nor is this the sum of its blessings. By teaching men how much they have in common, by awakening in them the sense of harmony in all the varieties of knowledge, by honoring every kind of educated mind, by inclosing with its emblematic girdle every interest of cultivated society, it facilitates our progress toward that holy unity which is so touchingly symbolized in the words, "*One fold and one shepherd.*"

Of late years the disposition to extend the sphere of education has been intensely active. It is a marked and an energetic impulse; and though, like all impulses, it has been at times fitful and wayward, yet it is a movement in the right direction. Without doubt, it has vitalized the pursuits of knowledge by the introduction of more generous sympathies and a freer range of activity. It has added new territories to the old domain; and while the mountain summits are no loftier, the table-land has been raised higher. Of course, there have been hot discussions and sharp dissensions. Classical scholars, mathematicians, scientists, metaphysicians, the advocates of modern languages, have joined in the strife—regiments of the same army confronting one another; but the conflict can be only temporary. It is a question, at last, of mere relativity and methodic adjustment. The instincts of cultivated intellect may be trusted to settle this debate; for if any thing in this world may be relied on to regulate itself by the principles of sound philosophy, it is education.

Let us take an illustrative example. If we approach the human mind from the material world, we gain access through the avenues of the senses to its awaiting faculties; and on this ground mathematics and physical science have the argument on their side. On the other hand, if we start from the opposite point and advance to the more spiritual instincts and sensibilities, classical language has the force of logic in its favor. It is a thing of method, no more. It is initial, and not final; preparatory, and not ultimate. The occult forces, which are latent in each individual, are subsequently evoked, and these determine the kind and extent of future development. So far, then, as one's personality is concerned, these invaluable modes of cultivating the mind are mainly tentative, their virtue lying in this fact, that they tend to give a student the consciousness of his capacity, and test his power to turn that capacity into practical ability. Aside from this, whether you take the intellect as operating through the senses or the sensibilities, it is most wisely trained by respecting its reciprocal action in these two distinct forms of thought. Unlike as they seem, they draw nearer together as they advance toward the goal of completed culture. Pascal was all the better in his "Thoughts" and "Provincial Letters" for his achievements in science, and Chalmers was the sublimer in his "Astronomical Discourses" for his knowledge of mathematics. One may attend Newton in his pathway to the Infinite, or Milton as he soars in his "singing robes" to heights untouched before, but in each case vastness of conception and grandeur of sentiment exalt the spirit.

Viewing the subject of education in one light, we have a single ideal; looking at it under other aspects, it has several ideals. If we accept the former, the mind, in its structure, in its self-contained powers, in its philosophy of growth, is the predominant thought; if the latter, the man in all his relations is the object of contemplation. Now, what appears best from one of these stand-points may not appear best from the other. The intellect and the man are not always on the same level. They touch different spheres; they often inhabit unlike worlds. Taste works one way and power another. Capacity has certain characteristics, and positive ability very dissimilar features. At times we see a great manhood by the partial forfeiture of intellectual development, and then again we see intellect draining off the vital resources of manhood; so that we cannot uniformly correlate the mind and the man. If this be true, it should teach us caution, lest we overestimate the absolute benefits of specific methods of education to the exclusion of all other instrumentalities. Until we get a comprehensive knowledge of the human mind, we must have conflicting ideals of education. Meanwhile, it is wisdom to be as liberal as possible, and to show the utmost cordiality in welcoming all modes and means of culture. The waters of the ocean rise into graceful clouds, float in vapory wreaths, bend in the rainbow, lie in long, level lines over the setting sun, moisten the lower air, and descend in nightly dews, and so make firmament and atmosphere a sea of blessing; while yet the same ocean, undiminished in fullness and unabated in majesty, bears the products of commerce around the globe.

When, therefore, we try to measure the final force of education, the scholar is lost in the man. Modes and methods disappear, as food and air vanish out of the blood. What remains is what has been assimilated: bone and muscle, heat in the lungs, light in the eye—these are results. Of this, then, we may rest assured, that only noble men can do noble work; and to have this nobility, we must give truth an ample sphere—such a one as embraces every element of freedom and every constituent of magnanimity. Faith in men as they are must precede faith in men as they may become, and this faith is the soul of education. Raise your platform a few inches, and where are your multitudinous distinctions? Whether the flash of the lightning and the roll of the thunder are above or below you is a matter of altitude. If you shut up utility within the pitiful inclosure of earthly greed and gain, you put it beyond the pale of philosophy. So, too, when you confine beauty in the circle of esthetics, you destroy half its charms. Far wiser were the Greeks. Winckelmann says that "the best workman in the most humble craft might succeed in rendering his name immortal; and we are told that the Greeks were accustomed to pray the gods that their memories might never die." You may ask of utility, "*Why was this waste made?*" with the same sort of pretext that you ask it of beauty, and in each case the question comes from the heart of Judas. Utility may be spiritual, as well as worldly; so may beauty. Each is capable of visibility and invisibility. Both may do God's work; and this is the stamp of their excellence; for the skill and toil that prepared the alabaster box of ointment have their place and reward in God's kingdom, as well as the tenderness of Mary when she made it an offering to her Lord.

How wisely, how beautifully the Lord Jesus reconciled these seeming contrarieties! You may view him as coming to man on the two sides of his nature, the spiritual and the material. Each of these his hand touched; against each of them his holy heart throbbed. Our twofold life and its strange interblendings were ever under his thoughtful eye; nor did he for an instant overlook the needs of the one or of the other. Man, in the serene light of his omniscience, was the fallen image of God and the fallen image of the universe. Inasmuch as the two are closely and vitally interlaced, and are in union for the sake of a union higher than we now understand, he gave to each its rightful place and just consideration. To restore him to moral law, that he might know, and love, and serve God as his Father; to restore him to physical law, that he might possess and enjoy the material universe as his home and empire, he taught, labored, healed, suffered, died. Drawing near to man in that large section of his nature which language represents, and of which it is the only interpreter, you can easily see why St. John should designate him as the "*Word.*" Nor can language ever need an advocate while that first chapter of the fourth Gospel stands in the forefront of Christian evidences. Apart from its immediate and divine purpose, it is an unanswerable argument in behalf of the profound study of language, whether regarded as a means of outward communication or as an introversive instrument to quicken and call forth the deepest intuitions of our moral being.

Turn to another aspect of the Redeemer's life. The "Word" was also the Worker, and in the same breath he spoke of "words" and "works" as though they were one. One indeed they were in him, but to us they belong to different realms. To show his infinite love for man, as dwelling on the earth, subjected to sorrow, and tortured by evils, and preyed on by demons, he wrought miracles to bless, and cheer, and save; out of his living heart flowed those streams of beneficence that watered his native land, as out of his dying heart there afterward issued the blood of a world's redemption. Not for the sake of their evidential force only, nor for the sole benefit of those immediately interested, did he multiply bread, and heal the sick, and walk the waters of the Galilean sea. Beyond their instant purpose they had a far-reaching intent, and in this end they expressed their highest import; for he designed to teach that these wonders contained seminal influences which, in other climes and under fairer skies, should germinate a hundred-fold. Miracles were they then, and their moral might and glory are prolonged even yet. Wherever art and science call to their aid the supreme agencies of natural law, and employ them in a ministration of Christian sympathy and helpfulness, there the divine

Spirit in these miracles is repeated; there the ancient majesty of goodness comes back again unalienated; and there the eye softens into the same sweet stillness, and the ready hand imitates its holy Exemplar.

Believe it, friends, believe it: the Son of God is yet in our midst. In his house on this earth are "*many mansions*," and they are luminous with his presence. See all around you scientific agriculture lessening toil and cheapening food; see machinery increasing production; see the auxiliaries to industry; see the progress of the medical art in soothing pain, checking epidemics, and rescuing men from the arms of death; and see the myriad ships that sail in the resplendent wake of those footsteps that trod the waves of the Lake of Gennesaret. "*I will not leave you comfortless;*" and here is one of the manifold fulfillments. Here, too, is the harmony between those studies and pursuits which consult the wants of the inward and outward man; and here, finally, is the highest of proofs that education and culture must be many-sided to do Christ's work in Christ's world.

It must be confessed, however, that we have made small progress in attaining this ideal. Unfortunately for the advancement of our race, the mass of men—even our advanced thinkers—are as fatally bent on rejecting Christ in providence as in the Cross of Calvary. "*What have we to do with thee, thou Jesus of Nazareth?*" is the oft-uttered cry of the spirit possessing the carnal mind. Sometimes, in the blind homage paid to material law, then in the fierce struggles of worldly competition, now in the frigid conclusions of logic, and then in the outbursts of frantic passion, this rebellious exclamation repeats its profane unbelief. Alluding to certain evils connected with "Progress," Froude speaks of "a public confession of despair of human nature;" nor indeed can we see how any other conclusion than "despair" can be reached when Christ, as the Head of humanity, is disowned. Man, as the child of Providence, never appeared to such advantage as now. But, amid this growing splendor, the question forces itself on us, "*What manner of man is this, that even the winds and the sea obey him?*"

"*The winds and the sea*" do truly "*obey him;*" nay, all things are beginning to bow down under his lordly rule. Find man where you will, he is girded with power. In the magnificent laboratory of the universe he unlooses new and prodigious forces to do his proud behests. Backed by inventions and discoveries, he has boundless scope for every sort of intelligent energy, so that he has well-nigh correlated himself with the globe he occupies. But, after all, what is he? Look for your answer in the gross worldliness everywhere abounding; in the fearful decay of obedience to authority, of loyalty to love, of fidelity in marriage, of trustworthiness in business, of reverence for God. If you had the making of a man to suit these times—to fight his way to the high places of ambitious success, and win the renown of earthly triumph—you would give him wondrous activity of intellect, its powers compacted in an animal brain, every sense and every nerve disciplined to serve a despotic will. This should be his outfit: the cunning of the fox, the stealthiness of the snake, the eye of the eagle, the spring of the tiger, the strength of the lion; and these the weapons of his organized fatality.

"*What manner of man is this*"—this representative man of the saddest aspects of the nineteenth century? Study him, probe him, and then say whether art and science are not creating mind and muscle they cannot control; whether government is not liberating a force too audacious and too reckless for it to hold in check; whether the very successes of modern civilization are not arousing appetites and lusts which are too brutal for the puny arm of its restraint.

Fitly and most worthily were the words "*What manner of man is this?*" spoken of Jesus Christ. But this ideal Man —tell us of what virgin's heart he has been born; in what manger cradled; in what lowly toil reared; in what Nazareth silently nurtured. What sacramental Jordan baptized him? What wilderness brought him face to face with the tempter? With what woe and wretchedness, sorrow and shame, sin and guilt, has he been in long and weary conflict, bearing burdens not his own, and quickening and inspiring the hopeless spirit of humanity? Where are his Tabor, and Olivet, and Calvary?

But let no man despair—the modern Samson may commit suicide, but he can never throw down the fabric of Christian civilization. It is humiliating to behold the decay of sentiment, to see honor losing even its ancient prestige, and to witness the growth of a debasing materialism in the very heart of our most sacred interests. Notwithstanding all these painful spectacles, the advanced portions of the race have built themselves upon high vantage-ground, and never can they surrender the massive work of bitter centuries. Happily enough, the dangers from outside barbarism are extinct. The womb of the old Gothic forests is childless, and the breast of the Danube gives no nurture. The evils of the age are among ourselves, plain and patent; and, as they are internal and simply domestic, they can be met and managed. Despite of adverse signs, Christianity has been too long in the world, and too severely tested, to be permanently injured by any assault. It has taken hold of the instincts of the race; it has ascended from reasoning into reason itself; and though it may now be approaching another epoch of trial, it can be but an epoch in the eternity of its grandeur.

Is not this an hour of inspiriting hope to your hearts? On yesterday, amid the sanctities of the Sabbath, we dedicated this temple of learning to God. To-day, under fairest auspices, we inaugurate its work among men. Among the many witnesses to the presence and power of Christian civilization, the VANDERBILT UNIVERSITY this morning takes its place and begins its career. Whether it has "*five talents*," or less, committed to its keeping, none of us can know. The supreme thing is to acknowledge God in what we have, and put our stewardship to diligent uses. As yet the institution has no history; but yesterday and to-day ought to be prophecies; nor could it write better annals than to fulfill these prefigurations. The last years of this century are hastening to make themselves memorable in endowing institutions of learning. A new era has commenced in this order of beneficence; yet, among the instances of thoughtful bounty, not one has been better timed, nor more considerate of urgent need, nor more gratefully appreciated, nor likely to issue in larger good, than the munificence which has established this University.

If one follows the River Rhone from the Mediterranean to Lyons, from Lyons up the valley, and thence through the district of the Jura to the rocky gorge of the mountain-chain where the turbid stream forces its passage, and still on to the junction of the Arne, and farther yet till he sees it rush in proud swiftness through the Lake of Geneva, and on again to the western side of Mount St. Gothard, among the Swiss Alps, he reaches at last the Valley of the Rhone. There the glaciers lift themselves to the sky; and even on those summits, where winter chills the heavens, huge masses of snow are piled up, sublimity crowning sublimity, and splendor overflashing splendor. Far down underneath those compacted blocks of ice, the River Rhone glides from the solitude of its source, and gathers from frost and snow the impulse of its resistless waters. Like that river, the course of great events has often started in desolate places; like it, the stream of civilization has taken its rise, at times, among dreary mountains and remote fastnesses, and flowed long and far before its current blessed the world. Not so with the fountain which this day gushes forth in our midst; its waters are full of warmth and fertility, and they roll onward to the swell of their own gladness. And may it ever be, as the river which St. John saw in the vision of Patmos, "*clear as crystal, proceeding out of the throne of God and of the Lamb!*"

After another performance by the Band, the Installation of the Faculties took place.

Bishop McTyeire, as President of the Board of Trust, addressed the Faculties, all the members of which stood during his Address, at the close of which he delivered over the keys of the University to L. C. Garland, LL.D., Chancellor of the University. The Bishop spoke as follows:

BISHOP McTYEIRE'S ADDRESS TO THE FACULTIES.

It is with great satisfaction we approach this hour of installation of the Faculties of the University, which, though it be important, will be brief. His Excellency, the Governor, closely outlined the scope of our University. The two speakers who followed him declared the spirit in which we propose to carry on the University. It remains now for us to formally invest those chosen as instructors, teachers, professors. Thus far all is dust—convenient and elegant forms of dust it may be. Now is to be breathed into it the breath of life, that the University may become a living soul. It is to these scientific and literary gentlemen we look to give character to the University. For two years we have been building, piling one stone and one story upon another. *Pari passu* we have been gathering our Faculties. The Board has been censured by some for delay. The first professor was elected two years ago—the last one, two weeks ago. All that time the eyes of the Trustees have been going through the land to find men suitable for intrusting this work to. They felt that they could not afford to make a mistake in this matter. The time will come when the fact that any man is connected with the Faculty of the VANDERBILT will give assurance of his ability. Then the institution will make the reputation of its professors; but now the professors must make the reputation of the institution. Our four Faculties are now complete. They are before you, and I proceed now, by the authority and in the name of the Board of Trust, to install them.

Here the Bishop turned to his right, and addressed the gentlemen, who rose and stood:

MR. CHANCELLOR AND GENTLEMEN OF THE FACULTIES:—We congratulate ourselves that we have been able to procure your services. I will say of VANDERBILT UNIVERSITY as the King of Macedon said when his son, Alexander, was born, writing to Aristotle: "We count ourselves happy, for that a son has been born to us at a time when you may be his instructor." We think it providential and fortunate for this University, which has sprung out of a benefaction which we accept and acknowledge with gratitude, that it has come to us in the South when we may enjoy the benefits of your acknowledged ability as instructors and governors of youth. This high responsibility the Board of Trustees would now devolve upon you, in full confidence of your ability and of your fidelity; and, in token of this, I now commit to you the keys of the University.

Chancellor GARLAND responded as follows:

CHANCELLOR GARLAND'S RESPONSE TO BISHOP McTYEIRE.

PRESIDENT McTYEIRE:—This is a day which many of us now present have hoped for, and prayed for, and labored for—a day on which we should see inaugurated, under the patronage of the Methodist Episcopal Church, South, an institution where, in its halls and academic groves, we might see Learning and Religion walk hand in hand, the one shedding its enlightening, and the other its benign, influences over the length and breadth of the land; and where our sons might receive the largest intellectual culture without detriment to their moral habits and religious sympathies; and where full provision should be made for professional as well as academic studies, so that in no part of their training should our sons pass from under the fostering care of the Church.

You know, sir, on that cold and dismal winter day of January, 1872, in the basement of the Second-street Church in Memphis, where you and I, and others, were assembled in convention for devising the ways and means of establishing such an institution, how gloomy was the prospect of success. How hopeless did it appear to make an appeal to a down-trodden and impoverished people for the sum of five hundred thousand dollars, which was declared to be the least sum necessary for the incipiency of the measure, and how absolutely chimerical to expect from the same source the million of dollars requisite to crown it with success! But, sir, there was in our midst one spirit which did not quail, one breast which hope did not forsake; and if there be any man whose portrait deserves to hang on these walls by the side of that which has just been unveiled, it is that of the wise, the prudent, the brave, the gentle, and the now sainted, A. L. P. Green. Without him, we should have postponed, probably to an indefinite period, the matter in hand; but he encouraged us by undertaking, with the assistance of an agent within the bounds of each patronizing Conference, to raise the minimum sum referred to. If mortal man could have succeeded in this business, he would so have done; but the result proved how utterly hopeless was the task—how inadequate our resources for such an enterprise. Yet, God's favor was upon the work. He was devising means, of which we knew not, for its accomplishment; and, when all other resources failed, He put it into the heart of our noble patron, whose name the institution bears, to come to our relief, and to do for our afflicted people what they were not able to do for themselves. But for his timely aid, none of us present on that wintry day would have lived to see what our eyes this day behold.

Were our munificent benefactor present, I would tell him how by this act he has implanted himself in the affections of more than a million of grateful people, and how from their hearts go up daily supplications that the blessings of God may rest upon him—that he may be preserved in health and happiness long to live, that his last days may be his brightest and his best, and that when he shall be called to pay that last debt which we all owe to nature, he may, through the infinite merit of Christ, be admitted to an inheritance incorruptible, and that fadeth not away, in heaven. But, sir, this magnificent donation lays peculiar responsibilities upon a variety of persons—responsibilities upon you, the Board of Trust, of which it is not proper that I should speak; responsibilities upon the community in the midst of which this institution is located, of which I shall not speak now, as you have expressed the wish that I should do so more at large on some other occasion; responsibilities upon these young men who have come to enjoy the first fruits of this liberality, and of which I shall have many opportunities of speaking in the future; and, lastly, responsibilities upon the several Faculties of this University, which you have just now in form imposed, by the delivery to them of the usual symbols of authority. So late, however, is the hour, and so wearied are the audience, that I will speak no farther of these responsibilities than to say that we are all fully aware of the difficulty and delicacy of the task imposed upon us. But, with your forbearance toward our infirmities, with the sympathy and good-will of the public, and, above all, with the aid of Almighty God, without whose blessing nothing great or good can be accomplished, we enter upon our duties hopefully and cheerfully, promising fidelity to the trusts committed to us, and pledging our best exertions to make this University all that its founder and friends desire it to be.

After the Installation, a part of the following Inauguration Ode, composed for the occasion by the Rev. A. A. LIPSCOMB, D.D., was sung by the Choir, in Old Hundred:

INAUGURATION ODE.

I.

Beneath the temple's stately height,
Midst pomp of gold—midst pearls of light,
While priestly chant with incense blends,
The crown of empire lowly bends;
The toil that awed the list'ning air
Now vocal breathes with praise and prayer,
And flames ne'er seen in sun or sky
Their splendors flash on Israel's eye.

II.

The heavenward Alps, sublime and lone,
Echo but faint the thunder's tone;
The mighty sea but rolls to shore
The dying cadence of its roar;
But priests and people blessings share
Far richer than their monarch's prayer;
Though myriad hearts in one may yearn,
Answers more full from God return.

III.

Hath not this house been reared by Thee?
Thy thought, thy grace, naught else we see;

Thy hand did seal its corner-stone,
Long waiting till thy favor shone:
Take now thine own, and evermore
Enrich it from thy bounty's store;
Each hour shed light upon our way,
Each step advance tow'rd perfect day.

IV.

O Earth, thou footstool of the Throne,
This glory thine—thine all alone;
Thy throb in air, thy throb in sea,
Our pulses ask this day of thee,
That in the thrill of gladdened heart
Our praise of thine may be a part,
While, rolling far, thy anthems tell
What raptures high within us swell.

V.

Not like the stones which Jesus taught
Should prophets be, with judgments fraught,
If scornful men should doom his name
With curse of silence born of shame:
Nay, every rock within these walls
Shall answer back when Jesus calls,
Each marble block a tablet be
Of laws proclaimed, O Lord, by thee.

VI.

Here arts and sciences shall meet,
Bright, festal hours, their coming greet;
Here Faith shall stand, archangel fair,
Her diadem of grandeur wear;
Here Truth, a pilgrim wandering far,
Shall tranquil rest 'neath Hope's fixed star;
And Beauty touch with sandaled feet
The turf with Sharon's fragrance sweet.

VII.

We bless thee to thy toiling hours
Mid fertile fields and fruitful showers;
We bless thee to the love that hastes
To barren sands and arid wastes:
Go—noblest types of manhood rear,
Each brother-man to man more dear;
Go—fill thy measure of renown,
Then wreathe around the cross thy crown.

VIII.

O *Alma Mater* of the years
Beyond our day of toil and tears;
O *Alma Mater* of a race
Whose future glows with largest grace,
Gird on the old heroic might,
Battle forever for the right,
And dare to do and dare to be
Whate'er is great, majestic, free!

At the conclusion of the Ode, this dispatch from Commodore VANDERBILT was read:

NEW YORK, Oct. 4.—To Bishop H. N. McTYEIRE: We send greeting to you all. May your institution be ever blessed by the great Governor of all things. C. VANDERBILT.

The dispatch was received by the audience with great enthusiasm.

The Benediction was pronounced by Bishop DOGGETT.

RESOLUTIONS OF THE BOARD OF TRUST AND THE FACULTIES.

AT a meeting of the Trustees and Faculties, held immediately after the Inauguration exercises, Bishop McTYEIRE presided, and the Rev. ROBERT A. YOUNG, D.D., acted as Secretary.

On motion of the Rev. C. D. OLIVER, D.D., seconded by T. A. ATCHISON, M.D., it was resolved that the entire proceedings of Sunday and Monday be published in book-form, embracing the Sermons of Bishops DOGGETT and WIGHTMAN, the Addresses of Drs. DEEMS and LIPSCOMB, the Speeches of Bishop McTYEIRE and Dr. GARLAND, the original Odes, etc.

On motion of E. S. JOYNES, LL.D., a Committee of Publication was ordered to be appointed.

On motion of Dr. JOYNES, the thanks of the Trustees and Faculties were tendered to the Chief Marshal and his staff, and to the Organist and Choir.

CHARACTER AND DESIGN OF THE BIBLICAL DEPARTMENT OF THE UNIVERSITY.

BY THOMAS O. SUMMERS, D.D.,
Professor of Systematic Theology.

THE character and design of the Biblical Department of the University were set forth in a Discourse delivered in the Chapel of the University on Sunday afternoon, October 17, 1875, as follows:

"Search the Scriptures." John v. 39.

In entering upon the duties which lie before us, we find it necessary to vindicate the high rank to which we have assigned the science which is to engage our attention.

It has become quite common to put Theology in contrast with Science, confining the latter to natural phenomena arranged in systematic order. But there is no good reason for this. Theology is as much a science as Biology, or any other *logia* which engages the philosophic mind.

Our great lexicographer defines Theology, "The science of God and divine things—the science which teaches the existence, character, and attributes of God, his laws and government, the doctrines we are to believe, and the duties we are to practice."

This is the general view of Theology. But this science is divided into Natural Theology and Revealed Theology.

Natural Theology teaches what may be known of God by

the light of nature. Revealed Theology teaches us what we may know of God by the Holy Scriptures.

The term is used in both a general and a specific sense.

In the general sense, it embraces all that we comprehend in divinity, or religion—whether natural or revealed.

In the specific sense, it is one department of the great science of religion, which comprehends Theology in the proper sense, which treats of the being and perfections of God; Christology, which treats of the person and work of Christ; Pneumatology, which treats of the person and work of the Holy Spirit; Anthropology, which treats of the nature, origin, duty, and destiny of man; Hamartiology, which treats of sin; Soteriology, which treats of salvation; Eschatology, which treats of the four last things, Death, Judgment, Heaven, and Hell; not to note numerous subdivisions, such as Cosmology, Angelology, Demonology, etc., which treat respectively of the World, Angels, Demons, etc.

It is obvious that there can be no sharply-defined logical division of the Science of Divinity into departments which will mutually exclude each other. Any attempt at this would be puerile and vain.

From the importance of the subjects comprehended in Theology, it is clear that this is the Science of Sciences. It subordinates all other sciences to itself. Like Emerson's "Representative Man," it subsidizes all besides. Even the Atheist, who ransacks creation to prove that there is no God, is made to yield his quota to the Theologian, who has the true philosopher's stone, with whose touch he turns all the baser metals to gold.

Mr. Locke, therefore, is justified in his eulogy of this sublime science. "Theology," he says, "is a science incomparably above all the rest. It is the comprehension of all other knowledge directed to its true end—that noble study which is every man's duty, and every one that can be called a rational creature is capable of. This is that science which would truly enlarge men's minds were it studied, or permitted to be studied, everywhere, and with that freedom and love of truth and charity which it teaches."

When we say that Theology teaches the being and perfections of God, we do not affirm that natural religion, apart from divine revelation, demonstrates the existence and attributes of a Supreme Being. This subject will in future engage our serious attention.

Our business is primarily with revealed religion—collaterally only with natural religion. Revealed religion is positive, authoritative, demonstrative; and Hagenbach has well observed, "It can never be the object of a positive religion to prove the existence of God, inasmuch as it always presupposes the knowledge that there is a God."

There is nothing so peculiar in our condition, living in an age long posterior to the miraculous inauguration of the Christian religion, which makes our case essentially different from that of the Apostles and Fathers of the Church. They assumed, and we also assume, as a fundamental fact, the being of God. As Hagenbach says, "Christianity stood on the basis of the Old Testament idea of God—now purified and carried beyond the limits of national interests—as a personal God, who, as the Creator of heaven and earth, rules over the human race; who had given the law, sent the prophets, and manifested himself most perfectly, and in the fullness of his personal presence in his Son Jesus Christ. Consequently, the believing Christian needed as little as his Jewish contemporary a proof of the being of God. But in the farther development of the Christian system, it became necessary, on the one hand, that Christians should defend themselves (apologetically) against the charge of Atheism, which was frequently brought against them; on the other hand, they had to demonstrate to the heathen

(polemically) that their pagan worship was false, and consequently in its very foundation was a denial of the living God (Atheism). When, therefore, the writings of the Fathers contain any thing like a proof of the existence of God, it is either the spontaneous expression of religious feeling in a rhetorical and hymnological form, or it is intimately connected with other definitions about the nature of God, with the doctrine of his unity, or with the doctrine concerning the creation and government of the world. But the Fathers of this period generally recurred to the innate knowledge of God—*testimonium animæ*, λόγος σπερματικός—which (as they thought) could be traced even in the heathen, and on the purity of which the knowledge of God depends."

That is to say, they held that the pure in heart can see God. "God is seen," says Theophilus, "by those who can see him, when they open the eyes of their soul. All men have eyes, but the eyes of some are blinded, that they cannot see the light of the sun. Thus it is with thee, O man! The eyes of thy soul are darkened by sin, even by thy sinful actions. Like a bright mirror, man must have a pure soul. If there be any rust on the mirror, man cannot see the reflection of his countenance in it; likewise, if there be sin in man, he cannot see God."

This is as much as to say that, apart from divine tuition, no man can acquire the knowledge of God, because all men are born in sin. This is what the primitive Fathers meant by "the innate knowledge of God."

"With this," as Hagenbach says, "they connected, but in a popular rather than in a strictly scientific form, what is commonly called, The Physico-theological, or teleological, proof, inferring the existence of a Creator from the works of Creation. More artificial proofs, such as the cosmological and the ontological, were unknown in this period. Even

the more profound thinkers of the Alexandrian school frankly acknowledged the impossibility of a strict proof of the existence of God, and the necessity of a revelation on God's part."

This is not the place for a discussion of the necessity of divine revelation. On this point we could furnish abundant testimony from the ancients as well as the moderns—heathen philosophers as well as Christian divines—and the foremost laymen as well. Thus Lord Bacon, in his "Prayer, or Psalm"—a production unsurpassed in sublimity by any thing uninspired—uses this language: "Thy creatures have been my books, but thy Scriptures much more. I have sought thee in the courts, fields, and gardens; but I have found thee in thy temples."

Milton, who was a theologian, though not a preacher, says: "True religion is the true worship and service of God, learned and believed from the word of God only. No man or angel can know how God would be worshiped and served unless God reveal it: he hath declared and taught us in the Holy Scriptures by inspired ministers, and in the Gospel by his own Son and his Apostles, with strictest command to reject all other traditions or additions whatsoever."

Macaulay, in his review of Ranke's "History of the Popes," says: "Natural religion is not a progressive science. All divine truth is, according to the doctrine of the Protestant Churches, revealed in certain books; nor can all the discourses of all the philosophers in the world add a single verse to any of these books. It is plain, therefore, that in divinity there cannot be a progress analogous to that which is constantly taking place in pharmacy, geology, and navigation. A Christian of the fifth century with a Bible is neither better nor worse situated than a Christian of the nineteenth century with a Bible, candor and natural acuteness being supposed equal. It matters not at all that the compass, printing, steam, gas, vaccination, and a thousand other discoveries and inventions, which were unknown in the fifth century, are familiar to the nineteenth. None of these discoveries and inventions has the smallest bearing on the question whether man is justified by faith alone, or whether the invocation of saints is an orthodox practice."

Thus the *necessity* of a written revelation is affirmed in opposition to the proud assumptions of infidels of every class; and its *sufficiency*, in opposition to the boasted dogma of "development," whether as held by Romanist or by Rationalist. The Apostle Jude found it needful to exhort the Christians of his day that they "should earnestly contend for the faith once delivered unto the saints." It was "delivered," as a divine revelation, and "once," that is, once for all. Woe to Popes or Councils that add one jot or one tittle to this perfect system of truth! woe to Neologists who diminish aught from it! Hear the voice of prophetic antiquity: "To the law and to the testimony: if they speak not according to this word, it is because there is no light in them." (Isa., viii. 20.) Hear the voice of the Master, as it echoes down the Christian ages: "Search the Scriptures." This is the platform on which we stand. The Charter of the VANDERBILT UNIVERSITY recognizes a Biblical Department in this institution. The Bible, therefore, is to be our great text-book. We are to teach nothing not contained in it—at least, nothing that is contrary to it—nothing that may not be directly or indirectly proved by it.

But what a task is thus exacted of us! Biblical science is theology with a witness! It embraces all its departments.

Here is a book which we call the Bible—*the Book*, by eminence. We label it, "THE WORKS OF GOD." But thousands deny it this preëminence. They say it is a cunningly —no, not even that—a stupidly devised fable—as contemptible as the Talmud or the Koran—inferior to the Rig-

Veda or the Zend-Avesta—and no more divine than the Book of Mormon. Hence the necessity of Apologetics and Criticism, comprehending the Evidences of Christianity and Ecclesiastical History. We must prove the divine origin of our religion. We can do this. By God's grace, we will do this—so that every student leaving these halls may say:

Should all the forms that men devise
  Assault my faith with treacherous art,
I'd call them vanity and lies,
  And bind the gospel to my heart.

But this book was written in Hebrew, Chaldee, and Hellenistic Greek. If we would know what it contains, and especially if we are set to teach it to others, we must either depend upon scholars who are acquainted with those languages for the interpretation of the sacred oracles, or we must learn the languages in which they are written, and interpret them ourselves. Now, every one knows that it is not necessary, in order to comprehend the plan of salvation, or even to teach it to others, that we should understand the sacred tongues, because, with all its defects, our incomparable English version of the Scriptures, with Commentaries, and other helps, will enable us to acquire the knowledge of revealed truth, and to become able ministers of the New Testament. But in every age it is necessary that some should be learned in the original tongues, and it cannot be denied that it is a great advantage to every minister to be able to consult the sacred text in the very words which were written by the inspiration of God. It is superfluous to argue a point which all will admit—none more readily than those who deplore their lack of this ability. Hence the necessity of Hermeneutics and Exegetics—a knowledge of the principles of interpretation and their special application.

But as Theology is a science, it is necessary that the

leading truths contained in the Bible—scattered up and down through its sixty-six books—should be arranged in regular order, so that their harmony, and consistency, and relative importance, may be seen, and the effect of the whole may be realized. There can be no "Analogy of Faith" without this. Hence the necessity of Systematic Divinity.

But it is not enough that those who are called to the sacred office should understand the word of God, and be able to systematize its teachings; they must know how to impart the knowledge of the truth to others. Thus the Apostle to Timothy: "Thou therefore, my son, be strong in the grace that is in Christ Jesus. And the things that thou hast heard of me among many witnesses, the same commit thou to faithful men, who shall be able to teach others also." It is a great thing in a preacher to be able to "speak justly, readily, clearly"—as, with epigrammatic point, Mr. Wesley expresses it. To this end, there are few who do not need instruction, so that they may avoid any thing awkward or affected in voice and gesture, as well as any improprieties in the matter of their discourses. Hence the necessity of Homiletics.

But men may preach like angels, yet their ministry be comparatively fruitless, because of their want of skill, or tact, or zeal, in the work which belongs to their office out of the pulpit. What a work is that! What a world of wisdom does it require for its due performance! And how many ministers are there that can preach passable sermons, and yet are mere children among their parishioners! They *bungle* in performing the various offices of their ministry. They know not how to act when called either "to the house of mourning" or "to the house of feasting." Of such it is frequently said, When they are in the pulpit they never ought to go out of it, and when they are out of it they never ought to go into it. They were never properly taught their duty. If they had been duly instructed before they entered on their ministry—the responsibilities of the sacred office being properly impressed upon them, with a divine unction qualifying them for the same—they might have proved an honor and a blessing, instead of a shame and a curse, to the Church. Hence the importance of Pastoral Theology. There can be no controversy about the necessity of all these studies. The only question which can arise concerns the time and manner in which they should be pursued. In regard to this there is a difference of opinion.

Some think that if a man is called to the work of the ministry, he should enter upon it at once, and study all the subjects we have named in connection with his pastoral work. This may be best for some men. We are not disposed to take issue on the subject. Let those who are of this mind enter upon the work in the name of their Divine Employer, and study to show themselves approved unto God, workmen that need not to be ashamed, rightly dividing the word of truth. Many of our most acceptable and most successful ministers have pursued this course. We have no controversy on this point.

But there are others who think that they can learn better with a teacher than without one—better without the responsibilities and interruptions of the pastoral care than with them—better where they have books and other facilities for study than in places where they have them not. For such men we wish to furnish the privileges and advantages which they need.

There is abundance of precedent for this.

Under the Theocracy there were the "Schools of the Prophets," where the "sons of the prophets"—that is, their disciples—were instructed in sacred lore. They were thus qualified to become instructors of the people. God did not, indeed, confine himself to men thus scholastically trained for those whom he employed in the sacred office—as Amos, for example, "was no prophet, neither was he a prophet's son;" "but," says he, "I was an herdman, and a gatherer of sycamore fruit; and the Lord took me as I followed the flock, and the Lord said unto me, Go, prophesy unto my people Israel." It is safe to say that God never will confine himself to any particular guild, or order of men, when he sends forth laborers into his harvest. But it is not unreasonable to suppose that those who have been trained to husbandry will know better than others how to wield the sickle and guide the plow.

The apostles, indeed, were not learned in Rabbinical lore—which is what is meant when it is said "that they were unlearned and ignorant men;"* but then they had enjoyed two or three years' daily communion with their Master—had heard "the gracious words" of eternal life from his own lips—and finally had them all reproduced with infallible certainty in their minds by the plenary inspiration of the Holy Spirit. How small are all our acquirements, though we may have sat at the feet of Gamaliel, compared with their divine endowments! The last and greatest of the apostles had been thoroughly drilled in Rabbinical learning—and perhaps in Grecian, too—but what was all this compared with the plenary inspiration vouchsafed to him by the Holy Ghost?

Their successors in the sacred ministry, who had not their supernatural qualifications, prepared themselves for their important work by a careful study of the word of God. In the early Church men were trained for the min-

---

*"Οτι ἄνθρωποι ἀγράμματοί εἰσι καὶ ἰδιῶται. Wiclif: "That thei werein vnlettrid and lewid men." Tyndale: "That they were vnlerned men and laye people." Cranmer: "That they were vnlerned and laye men."

istry in ecclesiastical seminaries, which were multiplied in all parts of the Christian world.

During the Middle Ages monastic institutions were founded for this purpose—as, for example, Iona, Bangor, Oxford, Cambridge, in the British Isles, and so on the continent of Europe, and also in the East.

During the Dark Ages many of these institutions degenerated into hot-beds of superstition, and even immorality, and not a few became extinct. But at the Reformation a fresh impulse was given to the cause of clerical education, and the Reformers put forth strenuous efforts to supply the Churches with "a godly learned ministry." The Puritans were very zealous in this matter—not only in the mother-country, but also in America; and many are the monuments of their enlightened zeal.

Mistakes, indeed, were made by all the Churches, the principal of which was this: in many instances learning, or a show of learning, was considered all-sufficient, and men who were never converted nor called to the ministry were sent forth from theological schools as pastors of the flock of Christ, thus creating a prejudice against "the schools of the prophets." The Methodists, who will not tolerate a mere man-made ministry, naturally shared largely in this prejudice. The Wesleys and their clerical associates, of course, did not, as they had been trained for the ministry in one of the most renowned universities of the world; yet they infinitely preferred what was stigmatized as an ignorant ministry to mitered infidels and cassocked libertines, not a few of whom cursed the Church in their day. But they wanted "learning and holiness combined" in those who ministered in holy things. Hence John Wesley early inquired what could be done for the training of the preachers. Year after year the question was asked in their Conferences, and the answer was the same: Nothing yet; when the Lord shall send us men with means to enable us to found a seminary for preachers, then we will have one, but not before.

Wesley had a great horror of debt; and, besides, he did not wish to proceed in so grave an enterprise till the path of duty was made "straight and plain before his face." He did not want the camp to move while the cloud rested upon the ark! Earnestly did he desire to see this work undertaken before he finished his course; but, like Moses, he came to the borders of the promised land, but was not allowed to come into its possession. How would he have rejoiced if Providence had raised up for him a THOMAS FARMER or a CORNELIUS VANDERBILT!

But what was not granted to Moses was vouchsafed to Joshua. Dr. Bunting and Mr. Watson, on whom Wesley's mantle fell, matured the plan, and Providence raised up men with the means to execute it; and first Richmond was purchased and endowed, and then another, and still a third institution, to which "the sons of the prophets" have been sent, and hundreds upon hundreds have been taught the way of the Lord more perfectly in their halls than it was ever taught before since the days of the apostles.

At first prejudice, deep-rooted opposition, was encountered; but the wisdom and prudence which marked all their movements, and the manifest blessing of Heaven which rested upon all their operations, vindicated the policy adopted; and now if there be any prejudice, any opposition, in England, to the Theological Institution, it never comes to the surface.

Even the Primitive Methodists, who were supposed to be specially averse to progress in this direction, have their seminary for ministers, adapted to their peculiar character and wants, with the practical good sense which marks their Connection, and from which we may profitably take some lessons.

The Northern Methodist Church encountered still stronger antagonism; but the movement was not to be suppressed. We watched with interest the fierce contest, with no misgiving, however, as to the result. The men who led in the movement were no fanatics, no ultraists. They did not wish to force their views upon their brethren who could not see the matter in the same light with themselves; nor did they attempt to make a scholastic training a *sine qua non* for the ministry. But they were resolved that all young men who were called to the sacred office, and who wanted a better preparation for it, and could profit by the instruction which such institutions afford, should not go without it, or be forced to seek it from others not "of our faith and order."

Nothing succeeds like success! They have succeeded. We have yet to learn that those who have gone forth from their halls of instruction into the pastoral work are at a discount among their brethren—that the Bishops find it more difficult to get places for them than for others—that they are less efficient in the great work of saving souls. On the contrary, they are at a premium, as everybody knows. Indeed, this itself has been brought as an objection to the movement, that educated men are sought after by the people and by the appointing power in preference to those who are not educated. *Hinc illæ lachrymæ.* But we can forgive this wrong!

We have sufficiently indicated the character of the Biblical Department of the VANDERBILT UNIVERSITY. Its design is, as Adam Clarke said it was his in writing his "Commentary," to give a better understanding of the sacred Scriptures than young ministers can acquire without some man to guide them. My honored colleagues, who will have to bear the burden and heat of the day, will instruct you, my young brethren, in all that you need to know in Hermeneutical and Exegetical Science—in Homiletical and Pastoral Theology—and if I can render you any aid in Systematic Divinity, as far as may be compatible with other duties, and as my limited acquirements will allow, I shall do it, in the name of God, with all my heart and soul; and I can assure you it will be a labor of love.

I shall endeavor to assist you in your study of the great standards of our faith—the Bible—"first, middle, and without end," like its Divine Author. Then, for the better study of the sacred volume, we shall endeavor to master those great monuments of Christian antiquity, the Three Creeds—the Apostles', the Niceno-Constantinopolitan, and that miscalled the Athanasian—all of which we cordially indorse, excepting the interpolated clause in the first, of the descent into hell, which may be interpreted in an innocent sense, but which is sometimes perverted to a sinister use, and which is therefore eliminated from our recension of that symbol; and the damnatory clauses in the Athanasian, which are so foreign from the genius of the gospel. The *Filioque* in the Niceno-Constantinopolitan we admit, though we cannot justify its interpolation by the Latins.

But these three great Creeds—especially the so-called Apostles' Creed, the Creed of our baptism, the Creed of Christendom—we consider invaluable monuments of orthodox Christian antiquity, and shall use them accordingly.

Of equal importance, in its place, is the Catechism of the Church—of course, I allude to what is known as the "Second Wesleyan Catechism." This is one of our recognized standards, and well does it deserve this distinction. It was digested from the Catechisms of the Churches of England and Scotland and Wesley's "Instructions," by that ripe theologian, Richard Watson, by appointment of the British Conference, and has received the sanction of universal

Methodism. What a blessing it would be if every minister knew by heart this good form of sound words!

But, as seems meet and proper, we shall make our Confession the grand text of this Department. Our Twenty-five Articles—at least, twenty-four of them—were prepared for the Methodist Episcopal Church in America by John Wesley himself. He judiciously abridged them from the Thirty-nine Articles of the Church of England. Though we do not expect the laity (much as it may be desired) to study and formally subscribe this Confession, yet we do expect the ministry to do so. And no one can minister at a Methodist altar in any part of the world who does not profess to believe these Articles.

But it is necessary, in order to a rational belief, that there should be an understanding of them. To this end, we must inquire into their origin—what gave birth to particular articles and special clauses—the meaning of the terms employed, the Scripture proofs of the positions assumed, the objections of adversaries and how they are to be met, and the practical uses of the doctrines advanced. No sane man can deny the reasonableness of all this.

All that we have said on this subject is in the spirit of that exquisitely beautiful and highly suggestive passage in John Wesley's Preface to his Sermons: "I have thought I am a creature of a day, passing through life as an arrow through the air. I am a spirit come from God, just hovering over the great gulf; till a few moments hence, I am no more seen! I drop into an unchangeable eternity! I want to know one thing, the way to heaven: how to land safe on that happy shore. God himself has condescended to teach the way; for this very end he came from heaven. He hath written it down in a book! O give me that book! At any price give me the book of God! I have it: here is knowledge enough for me. Let me be *homo unius libri.*

Here, then, I am, far from the busy ways of men. I sit down alone: only God is here. In his presence I open, I read, this book; for this end, to find the way to heaven. Is there a doubt concerning the meaning of what I read? Does any thing appear dark or intricate? I lift up my heart to the Father of lights. Lord, is it not thy word, 'If any man lack wisdom, let him ask of God?' Thou 'givest liberally and upbraidest not.' Thou hast said, 'If any be willing to do thy will, he shall know.' I am willing to do; let me know thy will. I then search after, and consider parallel passages of Scripture, 'comparing spiritual things with spiritual.' I meditate thereon, with all the attention and earnestness of which my mind is capable. If any doubt still remains, I consult those who are experienced in the things of God; and then the writings whereby, being dead, they yet speak. And what I thus learn, that I teach."

"Blessed Lord, who hast caused all Holy Scriptures to be written for our learning, grant that we may in such wise hear them, read, mark, learn, and inwardly digest them, that by patience and comfort of thy holy word, we may embrace and ever hold fast the blessed hope of everlasting life, which thou hast given us in our Saviour Jesus Christ. Amen."

www.ingramcontent.com/pod-product-compliance
Lightning Source LLC
LaVergne TN
LVHW021426110826
845150LV00007B/2108

* 9 7 8 1 4 2 5 5 0 7 2 5 1 *